Exploring
BOURNEMOUTH
COAST PATH

Leigh Hatts

COUNTRYSIDE BOOKS
NEWBURY BERKSHIRE

COUNTRYSIDE BOOKS
3 Catherine Road
Newbury, Berkshire

To view our complete range of books,
please visit us at
www. countrysidebooks co.uk

ISBN 1 85306 908 6

Photographs by the author
Cover picture of Bournemouth
supplied by Derek Forss

Produced through MRM Associates Ltd., Reading
Typeset by Jean Cussons Typesetting, Diss, Norfolk
Printed by Arrowsmith, Bristol

Contents

Introduction

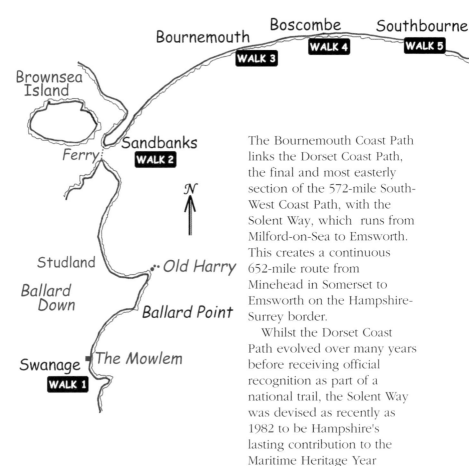

The Bournemouth Coast Path links the Dorset Coast Path, the final and most easterly section of the 572-mile South-West Coast Path, with the Solent Way, which runs from Milford-on-Sea to Emsworth. This creates a continuous 652-mile route from Minehead in Somerset to Emsworth on the Hampshire-Surrey border.

Whilst the Dorset Coast Path evolved over many years before receiving official recognition as part of a national trail, the Solent Way was devised as recently as 1982 to be Hampshire's lasting contribution to the Maritime Heritage Year festivities.

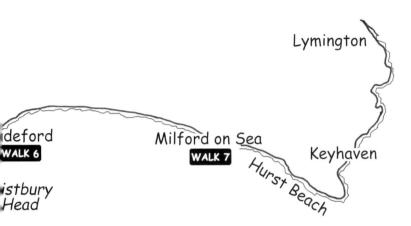

In 1985, when Countryside Books published my guide to the
Bournemouth Coast Path, the Sandbanks to Milford-on-Sea gap was
bridged. This new edition appears during the national maritime
celebration 'SeaBritain 2005' marking the 200th anniversary of the Battle
of Trafalgar. Lord Nelson's ship HMS *Victory* is on the Solent Way at
Portsmouth.

Since its launch in 1985, the Bournemouth Coast Path has been
recognised in numerous guides as an established route. In 2003 the
route was designated as part of the E9 European Coastal Path and an
inaugural ceremony took place on the Bournemouth Coast Path at
Sandbanks, in the garden at the junction of Banks and Shore roads
where a plaque can now be seen.

The E9 will run for 3,125 miles from Capo de São Vincente in Portugal
to Narva-Jöesuu in Estonia. Sections of coastal path in Portugal and
Spain are still under development but in France there are stretches of
continuous path between Sare and Contaut using the Arcachon and Cap-
Ferret ferry. The path also follows the coast of Belgium, Holland and
Germany to join the Baltic coast and includes the Polish and Russian
borders. Paths through Russia, Latvia and Lithuania have yet to be
established but much of the Estonia route is complete.

The British section is the 449 miles from Plymouth to Dover
embracing the South-West Coast Path, the Bournemouth Coast Path, the

Solent Way, the Staunton Way, the South Downs Way, the 1066 Country Walk and the Saxon Shore Way.

The Bournemouth Coast Path is full of varied interest with two natural harbours, ferries, woods, high cliffs and some of the finest views on the south coast. At the same time there is transport close at hand making the path an attractive proposition both for those wishing to explore only short stretches of coastline, and those walking longer sections of the path.

The Isle of Wight is a constant presence along the way, being viewed first from the west across Swanage Bay and finally from the north across the Solent. Marconi was in touch by very early radio with the Isle of Wight when setting up his experimental radio stations on the coast at both Sandbanks and Bournemouth. Edward VII was familiar with Bournemouth's East Cliff, Highcliffe Castle and Milford-on-Sea. His friend Lillie Langtry also knew both Bournemouth and Milford-on-Sea.

A recurring name along this coast is that of the artist Paul Nash who lived for a time at Swanage whilst writing, drawing and exploring Dorset. He died at Boscombe having just completed, in his cliff-top bedroom, a watercolour of the view, which included a typical Bournemouth shelter above Honeycombe Chine. The new winter alternative route round Christchurch Harbour means that the Bournemouth Coast Path now passes Christchurch Priory where Paul's great uncle Zachary was vicar in the 19th century. Nash died above Boscombe Chine which is just one of twelve of these valleys, known sometimes as a chine or, as you walk east, a bunny.

This new guide includes the original clifftop Bournemouth Coast Path route in Poole Bay for those who do not wish to be confined to the promenade which the new E9 designates as the main route for the Bournemouth stretches. The old cliff route affords the best panoramic views and the chance to explore the chines and rich coastal history.

There have been some improvements in path quality and waymarking since 1985. The opening of Highcliffe's Rothesay Wood footpath in March 2004 followed more than 20 years of numerous attempts to link Steamer Point Woods to Highcliffe Castle's grounds. Walkers no longer have to go down the high cliff to the beach for just a few yards. The diversion across the golf course between Barton-on-Sea and Becton Bunny has become unnecessary as a path now runs east along the cliff as it drops dramatically towards the Bunny. Meanwhile, however, the cliff at Barton-on-Sea continues to crumble especially at its western end near Chewton Bunny.

Many of the drawings by my father Ken Hatts have been retained from the first edition. It is interesting that only two proved to be unsuitable. One was the Pier Approach in Bournemouth where the swimming baths have given way to the IMAX building and the other is rural Taddiford Gap, all the wartime dragon's teeth having now toppled into the sea.

Using this guide

Included in this book are details of routes beyond each end of the Bournemouth Coast Path. These are the last few miles of the Dorset Coast Path from Swanage and the first few miles of the Solent Way to Lymington. This creates a 37-mile route which can be walked over a period of a few days from one base such as Bournemouth using the good bus and rail services. The directions are written from west to east to make the guide compatible with the majority of Dorset Coast Path guides.

For those wishing to reach the start of each section by car, there is parking available nearby and use can then be made of the good public transport links to return to your car. Details of the relevant buses and trains are given in each chapter.

The Bournemouth Coast Path website www.bournemouthcoast path.org.uk contains news of any changes to the route and transport information.

The maps accompanying each section in this guide are designed to give a simple but accurate idea of the route. However, some walkers may wish to carry an additional Ordnance Survey map. The entire route is covered by OS Outdoor Leisure Maps 15 (Purbeck & South Dorset) and 22 (New Forest).

Acknowledgements

I am grateful to both my wife Marion Marples and son James who have explored and researched the route with me over more than twenty years. James has also contributed the transport information.

Leigh Hatts

Hurst Point Lighthouse

Walk 1
SWANAGE TO SANDBANKS

The last seven miles of the Dorset Coast Path starts in the Isle of Purbeck's own tiny seaside resort of Swanage. The path makes a slow climb up to Ballard Down where on clear days there is a view of almost the entire Bournemouth Coast Path. After this preview, the way is through Studland village and along Studland Bay beach to Poole Harbour's entrance. American author Bill Bryson describes this route, mainly on National Trust land, as 'the most beautiful place in the UK' and travel writer Paul Gogarty, writing about Studland Bay, said 'It's hard to believe such places still exist in England; that miles of wilderness and open sky aren't mere childhood memories or adult fantasies'. It is also the area which inspired Enid Blyton when writing her Famous Five stories.

Studland Bay beach

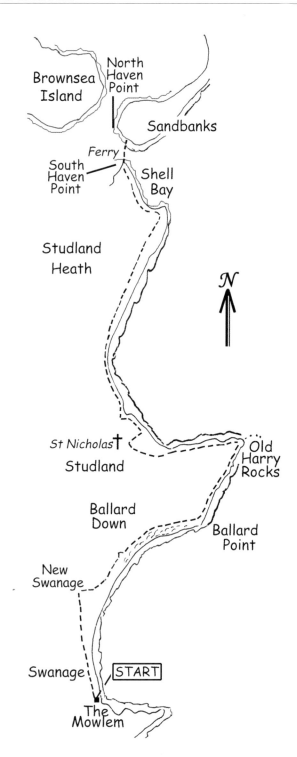

DISTANCE: 7 miles

TRANSPORT: Wilts & Dorset Bus 150 runs daily from Bournemouth Square to Swanage via Sandbanks Ferry and Studland. Wilts & Dorset Buses 142 and 143 run from Wareham Station on the London Waterloo-Weymouth line.

REFRESHMENTS: Swanage has numerous cafés and bakers. At Studland there is the Bankes Arms, open all day; the Manor House Hotel will serve tea; there is Manor Farm's tea room, open daily Easter-October until 5.30 pm; and there is also a shop and a beach café.

SWANAGE was reached mainly by boat until the end of the 18th century and today the area is known as the Isle of Purbeck. John Wesley's visit in 1787 was the result of his Southampton-Guernsey ship anchoring in the bay to avoid a storm. During the first half of the 19th century huge amounts of quarried stone were taken by sea to London by builder John Mowlem (founder of Mowlem contractors) and nephew George Burt who are believed to be the inspiration for John Galsworthy's 'Superior Dosset Forsyte' and 'Old Jolyon' in his book, *The Forsyte Saga*. On return trips,

The stone pier at Swanage

redundant London street furniture provided the ships' ballast and turned the town into 'London-by-the-Sea', with a fine collection of bollards bearing such names as City of London and Bloomsbury. Near the pier are two stone pillars from Regent Street; Wellington Tower near Peveril Point once stood at the south end of London Bridge; and Swanage Town Hall has the 17th-century Mercers' Hall frontage brought here when Cheapside was widened. Purbeck House Hotel, Burt's former home, has a collection of London relics, including pillars from Billingsgate, a Waterloo Bridge toll house, a Hyde Park Corner arch and tiles from the House of Commons members' lobby.

Swanage church

Swanage was Thomas Hardy's Knollsea and in *The Hand of Ethelberta* he set the wedding of Ethelberta and Lord Mountclere in the parish church. Hardy arrived here in 1875 from Bournemouth on Burt's new steamer service and, whilst completing the novel at West End Cottage in Seymer Place, he made Durlston Cottage, at the top of Seymer Road, into Captain Flower's home.

Queen Victoria came here as a 16-year-old princess and spent the night at the Royal Victoria (now the Peveril Inn and apartments) opposite Stone Quay. The queen's memories of the visit led her to send the 14-year-old future Edward VII to the hotel during his secret walking tour in 1856. The prince, travelling incognito with a tutor and equerry, was assigned only a sofa by the busy landlord who answered, when asked if the ballroom and the Queen's bedroom could be viewed, that he 'had no time for boys'. When the landlord discovered the visitor's identity he resolved to be polite to all guests whatever their appearance.

The railway reached here in 1885 just as the boom in stone waned and the beach was becoming a holiday feature. Although British Rail closed the line in 1972 it has been reopened by the Swanage Railway Project.

The Parade, next to the Mowlem, was built on the site of the Bankers – the spot where stone was stacked on the beach prior to loading. Artist Paul Nash lived at 2 The Parade from February 1935 until March 1936 whilst writing and illustrating the *Dorset Shell Guide*.

Church Hill, by the partly spring-fed mill pond, has hand-grooved paving stones and leads down to the Tithe Barn, housing a town museum (open May to September 2.30 pm to 4.30 pm).

✳   ✳   ✳

Join the Dorset Coast Path at the Mowlem which stands on the seafront at the end of Station Road. Turn north to follow the promenade (Shore Road). The sea is to the right.

After ¼ mile the road leaves the beach and turns steeply inland to become Ulwell Road. Keep past the Ferry Boat Inn and All Saints church (left) to continue along Redcliff Road.

Ballard Down

At a junction by the general store go right into Ballard Way. Keep ahead through the gateway of the Ballard Estate still featuring several old chalets. At a divide go right and soon the way bears left to run gently downhill. Before the end turn right by Greensands (number 24) to follow a short path to the cliff top.

On reaching grass, bear half left to a flight of steps at Sheps Hollow. Cross the ravine to follow the rising path on Punfield. Over the other fields to the left is Whitecliff Farm.

*　　*　　*

WHITECLIFF FARM   Paul Nash stayed here from October 1934 until February 1935 before moving to Swanage. From the coast path below the farm there is a view of the Ballard Down cliff which Nash included in his painting *Event on the Downs*. He once said, 'it is not until I think of Swanage that I recall the sea blue and beguiling'.

During the climb towards Ballard Down, the path rises and levels out and at one point it even runs slightly downhill for a few yards. The top of Ballard Cliff provides the best view over Swanage. Durlston Castle, on Durlston Head to the south, can be seen beyond Swanage.

*　　*　　*

At the signpost go right through a kissing gate and follow a fence (left). When the fence falls back, keep forward. It is important to keep on the path and not stray near the cliff edge.

At a stone, the rutted way merges with another path to briefly follow a fence (left). To the left is a view of Studland Beach and ahead is Bournemouth. In the sea below can be seen the chalk stacks known as The Pinnacle and The Haystack. The narrow cliff top path runs gently downhill, avoiding two dangerous promontories (the last of which has a natural arch), before reaching Old Harry Rocks.

*　　*　　*

OLD HARRY ROCKS probably take their name from the 15th-century Poole pirate Harry Paye. The other name for this landmark is Handfast Point with the gap between the mainland and the isolated stacks called

The Pinnacle and the Haystack

St Lucas Leap after a greyhound who jumped the gap soon after the natural linking archway collapsed in 1920. The furthest stack is Old Harry himself and until the great storm of 1896 (which swept away Brighton Chain Pier) the final gap was partly plugged by his 'wife'.

The rocks, still gradually being eroded by the sea, provide a refuge for the swooping gulls. Numerous ships have foundered off Old Harry, including the Spanish galleon *San Salvadore* – part of the scattered armada which had threatened Elizabeth I. Rabbits and salty winds help to keep the grass short and when the winds drop this is a superb picnic area with one of the finest views on the coast path. Studland, Shell Bay and the entire Poole Bay (including Bournemouth to the north) can be seen as well as Poole-bound ships moving between the smaller craft. The Isle of Wight over to the east is a continuation of this ridge of Purbeck Hills.

At Old Harry Rocks the path turns westwards and runs some yards from the cliff edge to pass through Studland Wood. Beyond the trees the now stoney path continues straight ahead for ½ mile, with no clear sea view.

Where the path divides (by the National Trust stone) bear right. Ignore the sharp turning to the right waymarked 'Coast Path' – this is an alternative via the beach. The way ahead is metalled for a short distance before becoming rough again. After passing the entrance to a lonely house (right) the now wider path runs downhill through a tunnel of trees to meet a lane in Studland.

Coast Path sign at Shell Bay

STUDLAND The tiny church, dedicated to St Nicholas, is Norman and has traces of Saxon work in the north wall. The building was saved from collapse in 1881 by careful underpinning. The pulpit is Jacobean and the processional cross is thought to have come from the Emperor of Ethiopia's chapel. Outside, to the south-west of the porch, is the tomb of Sgt William Lawrence who fought at Waterloo – the French inscription commemorates his wife whom he met in Paris during the Allied occupation.

Virginia Woolf first came to Studland in 1909 when she swam in a hired bathing costume. Later she stayed at 2 Harmony Cottages (opposite the Wesleyan church) and Harbour View behind Vine Cottage. Bertrand Russell met Olive Bell, another Bloomsbury Group member, at Studland, in 1910 and the following year Russell returned to spend a secret holiday with Lady Ottoline Morrell at Cliff End Cottage opposite the Bankes Arms.

A 1950s' figure was village policeman PC Christopher Rone, inspiration for Mr Plod in Enid Blyton's *Noddy* books.

The village cross, carved in 1976 at a Purbeck quarry, is on the traditional site and in Saxon style but the eastern side depicts modern life by including the Bomb and Concorde. The whole village is now in the care of the National Trust.

The tiny church of St Nicholas, Studland

Go right to pass the toilets and follow the lane uphill to the Bankes Arms. At the far end of the NT car park, a path on the left leads to the church. But just before this point go right on a path signed 'Fort Henry & Middle Beach'.

After a kissing gate, the fenced path runs down to a clifftop kissing gate. Go left along the cliff with the sea to the right. Soon there is a turning to the Manor House Hotel which can be seen inland.

*   *   *

MANOR HOUSE HOTEL The gothic-style house was built about 1825 as a seaside residence for George Bankes of Kingston Lacy, near Wimborne, who owned the village and beach.

*   *   *

After a short distance pass behind Fort Henry.

*   *   *

17

FORT HENRY, Britain's largest war-time observation post, was built by Canadian Engineers in 1943. Very early on 18th April 1944 George VI and Winston Churchill came here to watch the largest rehearsal by British and American troops for the D-Day landings. In 1971 Prince Charles, the king's grandson, made his first parachute jump over the bay.

*   *   *

The way runs through woodland. At a road turn sharp right to follow a lane downhill to Studland Bay. Turn left (north) to walk along the beach.

The northern end of Studland Bay beach

STUDLAND BAY has Studland Heath, a noted nature reserve, on one side. This area, dividing the sea from Poole Harbour, was once a thin spit but sand has built up on the east side over the last 400 years. This washed-up sand is blown on to plants such as lyme, marram and couch grasses which continue to grow through the new sand. Flowers also grow here in summer whilst the very old dunes have become covered with heather. The western bank of Little Sea (now freshwater, thanks to streams) marks the early 19th-century shoreline. Sea defences are now being abandoned as part of the National Trust policy of allowing erosion to take a natural course on the coast. The beach at the northern end, noted for its shells and seaweeds, since 1937 has been an unofficial nudist area. Bloomsbury Group artists Roger Fry and Vanessa Bell both painted on the beach.

*　　*　　*

After just over ½ mile there is the National Trust visitor centre which includes a café. Before the end of the bay, the route passes through the naturists' beach.

Afterwards the way bears north-west along the beach of the smaller and appropriately named Shell Bay to reach the huge and final South-West Coast Path marker at the end of the Dorset Coast Path at the Poole Harbour entrance.

*　　*　　*

POOLE HARBOUR & BROWNSEA ISLAND　Sandbanks Ferry operates across the entrance to the world's second largest natural harbour which includes the port of Poole. Just inside the harbour is Brownsea Island. The name was adopted at the beginning of the 20th century to replace 'Branksea' which had caused confusion for visitors travelling by railway who were tempted to alight at Branksome station rather than Poole two stops further on.

From Saxon times there was a chapel in the care of Cerne Abbey and when Henry VIII dissolved the monastery he built a castle on the island as part of his defence plan. During Elizabeth I's reign the owner was Sir Christopher Hatton.

The present familiar castle outline dates from the 1850s when William Waugh owned the island. He opened a seemingly successful pottery but, when a deputation of Poole shopkeepers arrived to invite Colonel Waugh to be their parliamentary candidate, they were received by his deaf wife who misheard them and pleaded for more time to pay their bills. This misunderstanding caused an unnecessary financial scare and the Waughs fled to Spain. Later, owner Charles Van Raalte managed, by buying land at Sandbanks, to become Mayor of Poole which automatically made him Admiral of the Port of Poole with the right to fly the official flag from the castle.

He and his wife entertained lavishly and welcomed Queen Marie of Romania and members of the Spanish royal family whose young princes and princesses often roamed free with the island children. In 1907 the first Scout camp was held on Brownsea as the result of a chance holiday meeting between Van Raalte and Robert Baden-Powell.

In 1927 banker's daughter Mary Bonham-Christie became the owner and expelled all residents in order that nature might take over the island. Horses and cattle were left to their own devices whilst she lived alone in the castle. After her death in 1961, at the age of 98, the island was handed to the National Trust with the castle becoming a John Lewis Partnership holiday home. Until 2003 there was no mains water.

The island, which has rare red squirrels and 200 peacocks, can be visited in the summer by ferry from Sandbanks.

*   *   *

From North Haven Point cross to Sandbanks by catching the ferry.

*   *   *

SANDBANKS FERRY across the Poole Harbour entrance is first mentioned 1581 and for centuries the ferry was provided by fishermen. A regular service started in 1880 and the present chain ferry service for vehicles was introduced in July 1926 saving 15 miles on the journey to Swanage from Bournemouth. This first 'floating bridge' was steam operated and carried about 14 cars. The steam was always hard to maintain in bad weather conditions and in 1958 a large diesel chain ferry was introduced. One night in October 1984 passengers had to be rescued when one of the two chains snapped and the vessel, carrying a bus, began drifting towards the harbour held only by the remaining chain. Two years later a build up of sand prevented the ferry from docking on the south side and a bus sank into the sand and sea and had to be salvaged by Royal Marines divers.

Walk 2
SANDBANKS TO BOURNEMOUTH

Sandbanks is the beginning of the Bournemouth Coast Path. This guide offers both the original coast route devised in 1985 and the official E9 which is a more direct route following mainly the promenade. After Sandbanks, the old route rises on to high cliffs with an occasional descent into wide chines. The word 'chine' is the name, found here and on the Isle of Wight, for the ravines carrying streams down to the sea. From the cliffs there are good views back to the Isle of Purbeck and ahead to Hengistbury Head with the Isle of Wight beyond.

The bay, stretching from Sandbanks to Hengistbury Head, was first called Poole Bay in 1810, the very year Bournemouth began its development. Ten years earlier Poet Laureate Robert Southey had walked along the beach from Southbourne in the vain hope of finding Sandbanks Ferry operating. In 1856 the young Prince of Wales walked the same beach from Bournemouth and managed to take a boat to Brownsea Island.

DISTANCE: 6 miles

TRANSPORT: Wilts & Dorset Bus 150 runs daily between Bournemouth Square and Sandbanks. In the summer there is also the Yellow Buses open top coastal service 12. Bournemouth Station is a mile from the Square, but bus 150 stops at Branksome Station.

REFRESHMENTS: Sandbanks Hotel (below Poole Head at the start of the promenade) serves teas; Branksome Chine Café (converted 1932 solarium) is open from 9.30 am to 11 pm and Argyll Gardens Café, just beyond Alum Chine, is open daily in summer from 10 am to 6 pm and on some winter days.

SANDBANKS The oldest house is the Haven Hotel which opened in 1887 and attracted Guglielmo Marconi who in 1898 transmitted from here some of the first wireless messages. In 1899 poet Robert Browning called it a 'salubrious spot'. Apart from the hotel and the coastguard cottages on the north side there were, in the 1920s, just corrugated shacks, old railway carriages and wooden chalets serving as holiday homes among

the dunes. Development
was slow due to a fear
that the peninsula would
be washed away. Tobacco
giant Sir Ernest Wills was
one of the first to build a
substantial house and
later John Lennon bought
a (now demolished)
house for his Aunt Mimi
who had brought him up
in Liverpool. Commenting
on the view of Brownsea
Island, the Beatle said, 'Of
all the places I have
travelled to this is the
most beautiful.'

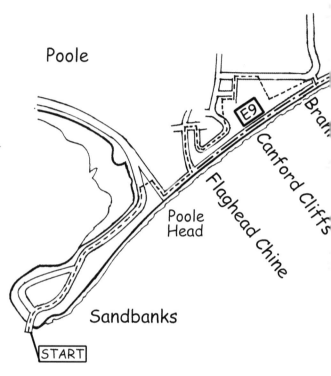

*   *   *

*From the ferry slipway
walk ahead to the
junction and go right
along Banks Road to
pass the Haven Hotel.
Beyond St Nicholas
Chapel and the shops,
the left hand pavement affords the best view of Poole Harbour with
the buildings of Poole visible opposite.*

*   *   *

POOLE The fishing port was established as an independent town in
1298. Today it handles cargo and passenger ships from Belgium, France
and the Channel Islands. The Royal National Lifeboat Institution
headquarters and Poole Pottery are also there. Just visible is the tower of
St James's church whose dedication is a reminder that this was an
embarkation port for pilgrims visiting the Apostle's shrine at Santiago in
Spain. The modern borough embraces Sandbanks and part of the
coastline.

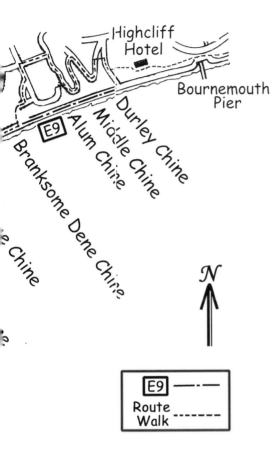

Highcliff
Hotel

Bournemouth
Pier

Durley Chine
Middle Chine
Alum Chine
Branksome Dene Chine
Chine

N

E9 —·—
Route
Walk ------

Just beyond the Sandbanks Hotel (right), go right through a small garden to reach a quiet section of Shore Road. Go right to meet the beach below Poole Head.

*   *   *

POOLE HEAD is the start of the 7-mile-long cliff running to Hengistbury Head beyond Bournemouth. Below Poole Head, where there was a battery in the 18th century, is the Sandbanks Hotel which incorporates Sand Acres, Sir Ernest Cassel's early 20th-century beach house. The first house on the cliff (above the line of white apartments) is Chaddesley Gate, built in 1937 for outdoor shop founder Oswald Bailey. At the very top is Little Fosters flats replacing Sir Bernard and Lady Docker's Tudor-style timber-framed bungalow demolished in 1989. Behind in Chaddesley Glen is the modern Church of the Transfiguration which first opened in 1911 as a wooden structure.

*   *   *

Turn left to follow the promenade. After about 450 yards the promenade passes over the site of Simpson's Folly.

SIMPSON'S FOLLY was a much-quoted reminder of teaching about building on sand. Between 1874 and 1878 John Simpson, a sea captain, built a concrete house on a sandy cliff. He lived there for five weeks before giving way to the Revd Hugh Pearson. Soon a storm washed out the foundations and by 1900 Poole Council had to blow up the dangerous structure. The 20 ft high pile of concrete became known as

Simpson's Folly, had steps built over it and lingered on the beach until 1961 when it became rubble for the new promenade.

* * *

| **E9** | *At Flag Head Chine the E9 continues ahead along the promenade.* |

The main route turns inland up Flag Head Chine.

FLAG HEAD CHINE, once called Beacon Chine, takes its name from the lookout which stood alone on the western side near Poole Head in the 1760s. Flags were flown to guide ships into Poole Harbour. Now, on the western side, are the grounds of St Ann's Hospital built in 1912 as the seaside branch of the Holloway Sanatorium in Surrey. The chine path links directly to Haven and Canford Cliffs Road which were smugglers' tracks leading to Kinson five miles away. At the top is the Norfolk Lodge Hotel, formerly Karkeel, which stood alone when built in 1886.

* * *

At the end of the chine path, go right into Flaghead Road and right again into Cliff Drive. At the far end follow the cliff top path which soon becomes separated from the road. The cliff path curves inland with Canford Cliffs Chine.

* * *

CANFORD CLIFFS CHINE was once known as Sugar Loaf Chine due to the now hidden hummock on the eastern valley of the Y-shaped chine. The path in the western ravine, sometimes called Smugglers' Chine, was used by smugglers on their way to Canford Cliffs Road.

* * *

The path becomes rough as it runs along the top of the old Smugglers' Chine (right). After a short steep slope the way joins a metalled path at a junction and climbs a short flight of steps. At the top turn right onto a rough path to continue along the top of the heavily wooded chine. There is a wooden fence (right) and after passing seats (right) the path bears left. At a junction of paths turn

Canford cliffs

right and soon join a path running parallel to the road (left). The path passes Riviera Court (left) before meeting a road by a junction near the Nightjar pub. Turn left up Ravine Road to meet the main road at Canford Cliffs village.

CANFORD CLIFFS was once the southern part of the manor of Canford near Wimborne. The Grand Parade of shops was built in 1909. For a time the chemist was also the sub-postmaster – one of only three people in Britain to combine the roles. The Nightjar pub is in the former stables of the Canford Cliffs Hotel which was bombed in 1941 and burnt out due to a lack of water. The Belgian Ambassador and Lady Kemsley were among those who made their escape in evening dress. A so-called Martello Tower, a gazebo built for Sir Charles Packe of Branksome Towers (see page 26), was the staff quarters.

Go right along Western Road. At Canford Cliffs library go right down the far side of the building to rejoin the cliff top. A path runs eastward and round the back of a sunken garden. There is a fine view over Branksome Chine to Bournemouth's seafront in the

distance. The way then drops down to a flight of steps and a curving path leading to the chine.

BRANKSOME CHINE 'Branksome' means a valley by the side of a hill. This area has often been compared to the French Riviera and in the 19th century it was claimed that, thanks to the pines, the climate was better than at Nice, Cannes, Menton and Montpelier. By 1904 the chine was said to be 'the Monte Carlo of the South Coast'.

The cliff top between Branksome Chine and Branksome Dene Chine, once called the 'Cap Martin of England', was until 1973 the site of the Branksome Towers Hotel, built in 1852 as a home for Sir Charles Packe, MP. The house became a hotel in 1898 and guests included Lloyd George, who stayed in 1921 as Prime Minister, the King and Queen of Afghanistan, the Duke of Windsor and the Beatles. Edgar Wallace set part of his novel *Mr Justice Maxell* here and Cyril Connolly included the 'steamy tropical atmosphere' of the hotel in *The Unquiet Grave* where he suggested that 'the pines here with their undergrowth of rhododendron and arbutus form the northernmost tip of the maritime forest which stretches from Hossegor, near Bayonne to expire at Bournemouth'.

Another hotel guest was Edith Sitwell who had spent part of her childhood at her grandmother's large house in the chine. The floor of the valley was declared open as a park in 1930 by Margaret Bondfield, the first woman cabinet minister.

John Betjeman wrote,

> *I walk the asphalt paths of Branksome Chine*
> *In resin scented air like strong Greek wine.*

E9   *Here the Bournemouth Coast Path and the E9 converge.*

Join the Promenade and continue walking towards Bournemouth. Keep by the sea for ⅓ mile to enter Branksome Dene Chine by the blue-roofed ice cream kiosk.

E9   *Here the E9 remains on the promenade as far as the cliff steps at the side of the Durley Inn at Durley Chine (see page 30).*

BRANKSOME DENE CHINE is four dry valleys. A rustic wooden bridge used to span the north-east corner near Zetland Court, home of Lady Wimborne. In 1893 her 18-year-old nephew Winston Churchill was playing on the bridge when he found himself cornered by both his brother and cousin and decided to slide down a pine tree. However, he fell 29 ft and his companions rushed back to the house to report that he had 'jumped over the bridge and won't speak to us'. He remained unconscious for three days and doctors from London discovered a ruptured kidney and a broken shoulder. It was during convalescence that Winston met leading statesmen and spent time in the House of Commons gallery. As a result he resolved to enter Parliament. Here in 1946 murderer Neville Heath, who features in Madame Tussaud's Chamber of Horrors, disposed of his victim's body. Viewpoint House, built in the 1930s on the eastern promontory, was for 33 years until 2003 the home of entertainer Max Bygraves.

✻   ✻   ✻

Climb the steps into the chine and at the far end bear half right to a long flight of steps signposted 'Sandbourne Road'. At the top walk through the rhododendron tunnel to reach the road.

Turn left to cross the invisible Poole-Bournemouth boundary and, before reaching the blue-roofed Cape Dutch-style house erected in 1932, turn left again at the junction. After passing flats, bear left into Alumhurst Road to follow the Zetland Court boundary (left) to the main entrance by a junction.

✻   ✻   ✻

ZETLAND COURT, once known simply as Branksome Dene, was designed by Edward Lamb and built in 1860 for Charles King, churchwarden of St Peter's in Bournemouth. Later the mansion became Lord Wimborne's seaside home. In 1890 the future Edward VII had lunch here having ridden over from Lord Wimborne's country seat at Canford to open the Westbourne Hospital. Early in the 20th century this was the home of Minna Cassel, sister of millionaire financier Sir Ernest Cassel. His grand-daughter Edwina was often a guest and in 1921 when penniless (due to her father's sudden death) she came here to borrow £100 from her great aunt in order to follow Lord Louis Mountbatten to India. Edwina caught up with him at Delhi where he proposed to her at the Vice-Regal

Alum Chine suspension bridge

lodge. Delighted, Mrs Cassel sent a diamond ring and a tiara as a wedding present. The house is now a retirement home. The Old Lodge in Alumhurst Road (opposite Alumdale Road) marks the entrance of the original driveway to Branksome Dene.

Turn right to walk down Beaulieu Road and continue ahead on the Alum Chine suspension bridge.

ALUM CHINE takes its name from a short-lived alum works opened here in 1564 by Lord Mountjoy of Canford. A long wooden bridge was replaced in 1905 by the present suspension bridge which features in Cyril Connolly's *The Unquiet Grave*. He wrote, 'Walking over the quivering planks I felt rooted, as in a nightmare, to the centre.'

Skerryvore, in Alum Chine Road at the top of the Chine, was the home of Robert Louis Stevenson from 1885 to 1887. His wife Fanny treated part of the chine as her own since their adjoining garden had no discernible boundary. In the only home the author ever had in England he wrote, 'The drawing room is a place so beautiful that it is like eating to sit down in it.' There he finished *Kidnapped* and, after a dream, he wrote *The Strange Case of Dr Jekyll and Mr Hyde*. John Singer Sargent came to paint Stevenson's portrait and a special chair was kept for Henry James. The house was bombed in 1940 but the garden is open daily (free).

The Tropical Garden (see below) was planted in the 1920s.

*   *   *

At the far end of the bridge turn right into West Overcliff Drive to follow the top of the wooded chine (right) back to the sea. Stay on the cliff top as the road treble-bends round Argyll Gardens bowling green and café. On the cliff there is the sheltered Tropical Garden.

Keep on the pavement as the road turns inland to follow the side of Middle Chine (right). Cross by the road bridge (built at the start of the 20th century before trees and rhododendrons were planted). Turn right to follow the east side of the chine back to the sea.

Before reaching the cliff there is a short cut (left) to Durley Chine along Cherry Tree Walk – a popular attraction at blossom time. The main route continues round the headland between the chines past two houses including Falaise (nearest Durley Chine).

*   *   *

FALAISE was the home of pioneer aviator Sir Alan Cobham in the 1950s and 1960s. The 11-bedroom house was built in 1913 and now, due to Sir Alan's travels, has a garden full of shrubs from around the world. Sir Charles Groves conducted the Bournemouth Symphony Orchestra in the garden when Cobham was BSO chairman.

*   *   *

Continue along the road which follows the west side of Durley Chine and passes the end of Cherry Tree Walk (left). Go right to cross the Durley Chine by a stepped path.

❋   ❋   ❋

DURLEY CHINE was probably named after Durley, near Bishop's Waltham, which was also owned by the Cooper-Dean family who lived in a Georgian mansion at Littledown on the edge of Bournemouth. The chine's stream is hidden in a pipe under the road.

❋   ❋   ❋

On the far side of Durley Chine bear right to reach the cliff top and follow the fence (right).

E9   *Beyond the trees, and in a corner, the E9 joins at the top of steps from the Durley Inn on the promenade.*

To the left is a wide grassed area. Stay by the fence to pass the West Cliff Zigzag.

❋   ❋   ❋

WEST CLIFF ZIGZAG, created in 1928 and rebuilt in 1984, is on the site of Joseph's Steps. These were made by Joseph Cutler about 1877 with timber washed ashore from the storm-damaged pier. For many years this spot was also known as Little Durley Chine.

❋   ❋   ❋

The cliff-top path briefly joins a road before passing the Highcliff Hotel.

❋   ❋   ❋

HIGHCLIFF HOTEL was built as a terrace of four houses called Highcliffe Mansions but shortly afterwards, in 1874, it was adapted to form a 50-bedroom hotel. Robert Louis Stevenson stayed for a week in

August 1884 whilst looking for a house (see page 29). The 'e' in Highcliff was dropped soon after the First World War due to numerous postal delivery errors caused by the existence of a hotel at Highcliffe (see page 69). The decision was made by the toss of a coin but until recently the old spelling could be found on some hotel silverware. With the addition of the eastern wing in the 1930s, accommodation doubled. In May 1940 a meeting of the Labour Party National Executive Committee in the hotel's basement led to Winston Churchill becoming leader of the wartime coalition. Clement Attlee was here as the then Labour Leader. After the war, Prime Ministers James Callaghan, John Major and Tony Blair stayed during their party conferences. In the grounds are former coastguard cottages, built in 1831, where Prime Minister Margaret Thatcher stayed during her party conference.

✳   ✳   ✳

Keep ahead on the cliff path which runs downhill past a cliff lift into the largest chine of all – Bournemouth.

✳   ✳   ✳

On the way there is the Bournemouth International Centre which was completed in 1984 to host party conferences and other national gatherings.

Walk 3
BOURNEMOUTH TO BOSCOMBE

This short straight section, known as the East Cliff, links the piers at Bournemouth and Boscombe. In 1846 when the Duke of Argyll spent two weeks walking among the young pines on the cliff he saw only squirrels. Gervis Road and Manor Road which run parallel to the cliff retain the remnants of that wood planted early in the 19th century by lord of the manor Sir George Tapps-Gervis. Building started just after this time and the mansions, which have largely given way to flats, housed Gladstone, Disraeli's Lord Chancellor Lord Cairns, and even the Swedish royal family. It was discovered in 2003 that green lizards, usually found in Spain or Italy, and sometimes a foot long, now abound on the cliff top.

DISTANCE: 1½ miles
TRANSPORT: Yellow Buses run to and from Bournemouth station.
REFRESHMENTS: There are several cafés near Bournemouth Pier, and Harry Ramsden's fish and chip restaurant and take-away is at the beginning of the promenade.

BOURNEMOUTH stands at the mouth of the long chine down which the Bourne stream flows. The mouth of the Bourne was an unpopulated corner of the vast parish of Holdenhurst, a Saxon village on the Stour river, when Lewis Tregonwell built a summer retreat here in 1810. His house survives as the Royal Exeter Hotel where guests have included the Empress of Austria who in 1888 granted the hotel the right to fly her personal standard on Sundays.

The church of St Peter's was designed by G.E. Street who was responsible for London's Strand Law Courts. This is the town's original parish church where Hubert Parry was baptised and William Gladstone received his last communion in church. Its Keble Chapel recalls Catholic revival founder and hymn-writer John Keble who died at Brookside, now part of the White Hermitage Hotel, near the pier. At the top of the churchyard steps is the Shelley tomb containing the heart of poet Percy Bysshe Shelley and his wife Mary who wrote *Frankenstein*. Her parents, early feminist Mary Wollstonecraft and William Godwin, also rest here having been exhumed from St Pancras, under Thomas

Hardy's supervision, to make way for the railway station. This is Hardy's Sandbourne which he described as a 'fashionable watering-place with its … groves of pine'.

St Stephen's was designed by J.L. Pearson of Truro cathedral fame. John Betjeman considered it 'worth travelling 200 miles and being sick in the coach to have seen inside of this many vested church'. The first wedding was a Lutheran ceremony when Prince Bernadotte married a lady-in-waiting in the presence of his mother, the Swedish queen.

Beales department store was, in 1885, the first ever shop to have Father Christmas in residence. A plaque in Exeter Road marks the site of artist Aubrey Beardsley's home in 1897, and another at Grantchester in Dean Park Road records that Rupert Brooke discovered poetry there whilst staying with his aunts.

In 1898, Marconi set up a wireless telegraphy station near the pier (see page 21). The Pavilion, on the east side of the Bourne, opened in 1929 and was the venue for many party and union conferences until the BIC opposite was built.

| **E9** | *The E9 continues along the promenade as far as Toft Zig Zag.* |

The main route continues up the wide cliff path at the side of the IMAX cinema. In the hedge on the left can be seen the old gateways to the cliffside houses which stood on the car park. One was the cliff entrance to Kildare.

KILDARE Fabian writer Beatrice Webb spent three winters at the boarding house when in her late twenties. Here she received in the post her first acceptance for an article and always spoke of the moment as the turning point in her life. In her upstairs bedroom she heard and saw the sea's waves which she said seemed to express first her depression and then her joy.

*　　*　　*

The path continues to rise past the back of the Royal Bath Hotel.

The **ROYAL BATH HOTEL**, designed by Augustus Pugin's pupil Benjamin Ferrey, opened on Queen Victoria's Coronation Day in 1838 when it was known as The Hotel. 'Bath' refers to the public bath which was at the bottom of the hill near the pier, and 'Royal' was added as a result of the Prince of Wales having spent a night here incognito whilst on a walking holiday in 1856 (see Swanage page 12). Later both Edward VIII and George VI stayed here before becoming king. The exiled Empress Eugenie had a surprise at the hotel when she noticed a cabinet from her boudoir at St Cloud.

In 1874 Queen Victoria suggested 'the very salubrious air of Bournemouth' to her new premier Benjamin Disraeli who had been unwell at Balmoral. He arrived at the hotel in November and found his first-floor accommodation so uncomfortable that he hired a sofa. When snow fell the rooms became very cold. But the Prince of Wales sent him twenty pheasants to supplement the hotel meals and Disraeli wrote to the Queen, 'The visit to this place, which Your Majesty yourself deigned to recommend, will turn out a great success'.

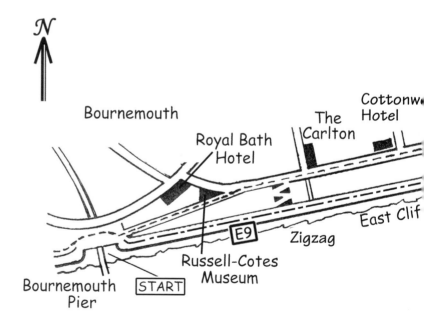

Other visiting prime ministers have included Gladstone, Asquith and Lloyd George. The dining room (based on the Egyptian Hall at the Lord Mayor of London's Mansion House) was known as the 'House of Lords' due to the London clientele. Oscar Wilde called it a 'palace'.

*   *   *

The next garden belongs to the Russell-Côtes Museum.

*   *   *

RUSSELL-CÔTES ART GALLERY & MUSEUM, formerly East Cliff Hall, was built in 1894 as the residence of Sir Merton Russell-Côtes who became mayor. The architect of this Italian Riviera-style villa was John Fogerty and in 1967 it was portrayed as Valentino's Hollywood home in the film *Valentino*. As Sir Merton also owned the Royal Bath, the Empress's cabinet is here (see above). In 1919 Queen Victoria's daughter

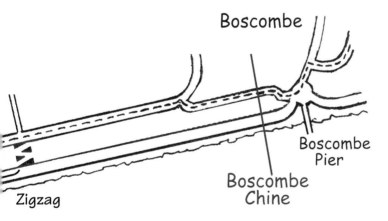

Russell-Côtes Art Gallery and Museum

Princess Beatrice and grand-daughter Princess Marie Louise had tea in Lady Russell-Côtes' boudoir within a few months of each other.

Since the house became a museum in 1922, royal visitors have included the future George VI (on his way to make his first speech), King Gustav of Sweden in 1970 and the Duke of Gloucester on the afternoon of 11th September 2001.

Russell-Côtes travelled widely and his Japanese collection fills several rooms. The art gallery, added to the east end, is noted not only for its collection of Edwin Long paintings but also has work by Gainsborough, Constable, Winterhalter, Landseer, Frith, Byam Shaw and Graham Sutherland. The most prized painting is Rosetti's *Venus Verticordia*.

The late Sir Hugh Casson described a visit as 'rather like opening somebody else's toy cupboard'. The almost perfectly preserved lavatories are by George Jennings who also improved the plumbing at Buckingham Palace. It is open on Tuesday to Sunday, 10 am to 5 pm (free).

The path joins the East Cliff Drive. On the left is Hinton Wood flats and the Miramar Hotel.

✳   ✳   ✳

Wick ferry

HINTON WOOD Sir George Talbot gave up his Grosvenor Square house in 1849 to live in the original Hinton Wood house on this site. 'Hinton' is the name of the hamlet on the edge of the New Forest where landlord Sir George Tapps-Gervis lived. With Talbot came his celebrated daughters including Georgina who founded Talbot Village, a model community on the west side of Bournemouth.

MIRAMAR HOTEL Writer J.R.R. Tolkein and his wife stayed here regularly in the 1960s as a plaque indicates.

*   *   *

Soon the path becomes separated from the road and passes the top of the East Cliff Zigzag.

*   *   *

EAST CLIFF ZIGZAG was built during 1908–9. Previously there had been winding wooden steps here called the Meyrick Steps after landowner Tapps-Gervis who assumed the additional surname Meyrick in 1876. Earlier this slight cliff indentation, with its easy beach access, had been known as Steps Chine.

*   *   *

Continue along the main path to rejoin the road at the East Cliff lift viewpoint.

*   *   *

EAST CLIFF LIFT, which once had cars in yellow Bournemouth Transport livery, was built in 1908 when the promenade was being constructed. Inland there is a view down Meyrick Road to the Bournemouth College clock tower competed just before the First World War. A short distance along the road there is a rare Penfold pillar box which has stood here (originally on the junction's north-west corner) since 1876.

*   *   *

Across the road is the Carlton hotel.

*   *   *

THE CARLTON opened in 1900. Regular guests included Princess Marie Louise and Princess Helena Victoria. Once they arrived to find that their jewellery case had fallen off the car's luggage rack. Lord Montgomery, who had discussed the D-Day plans with General Eisenhower at the hotel in 1944, often stayed in later life. In 1955, when the Conservative Party Conference was held in the town, this was the conference hotel and the scene of a late-night cabinet meeting called by Anthony Eden. Other guests include Gracie Fields, Anna Neagle, Bournemouth-born Virginia Wade and Terence Rattigan, who based a play on the Rattenbury murder in nearby Manor Road. More recently Prince and Princess Michael stayed a night and Princess Margaret lunched here. Once a guest put the hotel's reputation to the test by ordering the then little-known Omelette Arnold Bennett. The dish was quickly produced thanks to the chef who had been in the Savoy kitchen on the day it was invented.

*   *   *

Continue along the cliff with the sea to the right. Near the end of the line of hotels is the Cottonwood Hotel.

*   *   *

COTTONWOOD HOTEL is named after the Cotton family who bought the house from the Rothschild family who had built it as a holiday residence in 1889. The Prince of Wales is believed to have been among the many visitors. As a hotel the guests included the Asprey family of Bond Street fame. The original frieze and fireplace are preserved in the bar.

*   *   *

After the road junction a shelter marks the entrance to Toft Zigzag.

*   *   *

TOFT ZIGZAG The wooden Toft Steps were replaced by stone steps after a cliff fall in 1916 but now they have given way to the zigzag. From 'Toft' comes The Toft, now Toft Mansions, which stands to the east of the footpath running inland. Major Cornwallis-West (see page 78) lived there during the Second World War. The footpath leads to Derby Road where author John Galsworthy attended school between 1876 and 1881. Further along the road is Langtry Manor where 'socialite, beauty and actress' Lillie Langtry once lived and often entertained the Prince of Wales.

Here the E9 joins the main route.

E9	*Continue along the cliff path. The tall block of flats inland is known as Crag Head.*

*   *   *

CRAG HEAD The flats were erected in 1974 on the site of the original Crag Head which had been built in 1870 and survived until 1972. This was the winter home of Sweden's King Oscar II and Queen Sophie in 1881 when the king laid the foundation stone of the Mont Dore Hotel which is now the Town Hall. The queen returned in 1888 to host her son's wedding breakfast (see page 33). Stained glass in the staircase windows depicted the Swedish royal arms. Even the lodge has been demolished as it was considered to be out of keeping with the new building. One-time resident in the new flats was author Gordon Honeycombe who wrote his first books here after leaving newscasting.

Ahead, across the wooded Boscombe Chine, can be seen the Chine Hotel and the massive San Remo Towers (see page 44).

*   *   *

When the road ends keep ahead on the now enclosed path (where Beardsley was taken ill; see page 44) to follow steps down to Boscombe Pier.

Walk 4
BOSCOMBE TO SOUTHBOURNE

The once remote suburbs of Boscombe and Southbourne have expanded and merged to become part of the large Bournemouth conurbation. There are no more chines except for the so-called Honeycombe Chine, but the two miles of undulating grass cliff top, the remains of the once extensive sand dunes, are home to 600 sand lizards. At the far end is Point House where, according to Blur bass guitarist Alex James, you can enjoy 'a world beater' cheese on toast.

Boscombe Chine

DISTANCE: 2½ miles

TRANSPORT: Yellow Buses No 7 runs to Boscombe Pier and in summer open-top coastal service 12 links with Bournemouth Pier and Southbourne.

REFRESHMENTS: Brewster's The Neptune's at Boscombe Pier, Riva Café at Fisherman's Walk and Edna's, 29 St Catherine's Road in Southbourne, are open daily. Bistro on the Beach at Southbourne is open Tuesday to Sunday 9 am to 4.30 pm, and Point House, at the very end of the cliff, is open for refreshments in summer from 10 am to 5.30 pm.

BOSCOMBE CHINE was once known as Boscombe Bunny – still the local name for a chine in Christchurch Bay. Boscombe was open ground with hardly any houses or trees when Sir Henry Drummond-Wolff, local MP and diplomat, purchased the land between the chine and Sea Road in 1868. He developed the area as a rival to Bournemouth by building a thatched hut over a spring at the chine entrance and calling it Boscombe Spa. In 1874 the Chine Hotel was built above in Boscombe Spa Road and in 1888 work began on the pier.

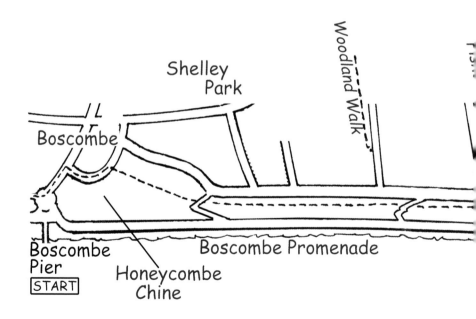

Owls Road is named after *The Owl* weekly newspaper published in London by Sir Henry and Lord Wharncliffe – hence Wharncliffe Road. At the top of Sea Road is Boscombe Arcade which opened as the Grand Continental Arcade in 1893 with the adjoining Grand Continental Theatre following in 1895. Stars appearing at this fine Victorian theatre, now the Opera House, included Sarah Bernhardt, Ellen Terry, Laurel and Hardy, Billy Cotton and Vera Lynn. Sir Henry Irving included it in his farewell tour, Marie Lloyd sang *'My old man said follow the van'* and Honor Blackman, made her stage debut there. In 1904 future Prime Minister Asquith, addressing a packed Liberal gathering, called for 'an Empire that would be worthy of the name'. However, this early multi-purpose centre had its opponents who placed a figure of the Devil on the building opposite.

The chine, now Boscombe Gardens, was still very sandy in 1896 when Aubrey Beardsley (see page 40) came to stay at the Pier Hotel (now replaced by The Point flats). He spent six months in an upstairs sea view room where each evening he sat between two ormolu candlesticks

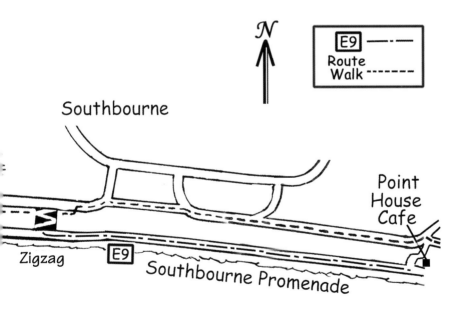

working on drawings. He suffered a haemorrhage near the top of the path to the East Cliff and on his tortured journey back to the hotel he drank some water at the spa. He was here when a 65 ft whale was washed up on the east side of the pier. Extra trains were laid on to bring sightseers and their children who used the whale as a slide until it began to give off a smell which penetrated inland. Later the skeleton was for many years a feature on the pier.

In 1946 another artist came here. Paul Nash (see page 13) painted the cliff view from his hotel (now flats) in Boscombe Spa Road just before his death there.

*　　*　　*

Turn away from Boscombe Pier to walk up Sea Road. After a short distance go right in front of The Point to go up The Marina. The road climbs steeply up the cliff to reach San Remo Towers.

*　　*　　*

SAN REMO TOWERS, by American architect Hector O. Hamilton, has 164 flats and was much criticised for its unusual windows when completed in 1938. However, the building's roof soon proved a suitable location for an anti-aircraft battery which shot down a low-flying German plane.

*　　*　　*

Turn right to enter Boscombe Cliff Gardens and follow the cliff-top fence. There is a view down into Honeycombe Chine.

*　　*　　*

HONEYCOMBE CHINE takes its name from the cliff's once honeycomb appearance caused by wind and rain scouring out the sand and leaving only clay. The extra 'e' in Honeycombe is a mystery. In the second half of the 19th century this alcove was known as Shelley Chine after Lady Shelley's summerhouse here.

*　　*　　*

San Remo Towers

Keep with the fence which curves round to a fine viewpoint looking west towards Bournemouth. The way then becomes separated from the cliff edge by bushes. Keep along the metalled path by the lawn. At the far end of the gardens, just before a gateway, take the right fork to reach the open cliff top.

Follow the path over a crosspath (leading to Manor Steps Zig Zag) to the cliff-top fence. Here there is a good view of the way ahead along the curving cliff to Hengistbury Head. Inland, where there is a gap in the line of buildings, is the unfenced and wooded garden of Shelley Park.

*   *   *

Shelley Park

SHELLEY PARK Sir Percy Shelley, son of the poet Percy Bysshe Shelley, moved here in 1849 for the sake of his sick mother Mary (see page 32) who died before moving in. Percy's wife kept the drowned poet's shrivelled heart, snatched from his beach cremation in Viareggio, in a room known as the Sanctum. Here she built up a collection of relics and documents which became the basis of the Bodleian Library's Shelley Collection. The house has a theatre where guests of the Shelleys made up audiences and often included R.L. Stevenson's wife. Percy painted the stage drop scene showing his father's last home, Casa Magni in Italy. One evening, when the entertainment was *The Wreck Ashore*, an unconscious Norwegian sailor was carried into the house after his ship had been driven on to the beach. Next morning he had disappeared before anyone else awoke. The garden is now a park.

✻   ✻   ✻

Continue along the cliff path which soon moves away from the fence. Further on there is a view of Boscombe Cliff Bowling Club which hides the end of Woodland Walk.

✻   ✻   ✻

WOODLAND WALK runs inland to splendid gates next to a lodge at Boscombe's main road. Much of the path is the former carriageway of Wentworth Lodge, the seaside home of Lord Portman. The house, built in 1873 and one of the first to be constructed of concrete, survives in College Road as Wentworth College. Lord Portman, whose main home was Bryanston near Blandford, maintained a large kitchen garden here. Nearby Portman Ravine was the beach access point for the house.

Boscombe cliffs

Continue along the cliff to meet a path, opposite steps, leading to Portman Ravine. Go right and take the left fork to return to the cliff top fence. Keep on to pass a children's playground and the Riva Café. At the side of the Commodore Hotel there is Fisherman's Walk.

FISHERMAN'S WALK The very straight ¼ mile long path led to wooden cliff steps and so was probably used by fishermen. This was the direct route to the beach from Stourfield House which was built in 1766 with a view over the Stour Valley. The Georgian mansion (just above Ravenscourt Road until demolished in 1990) was, from 1795 to 1800, the last home of the Countess of Strathmore. Her maiden name of Bowes led to bows being included on the arms of her great great grand-daughter the late Queen Mother. Lady Strathmore came here to avoid her second husband who had kidnapped her in an Oxford Street shop and held her prisoner in a castle. Whilst here she had visits from poet Robert Southey who lived near Christchurch and enjoyed browsing in her library. On her death here in 1800 she was clothed in her wedding dress before being taken to Westminster Abbey.

*   *   *

Keep away from the cliff lift (right) and take the higher path near the road. The rising path, which divides to pass a shelter, later runs by the cliff top. When level with the Spyglass & Kettle do not be tempted on to the higher path but keep to the path which runs downhill to the zigzag entrance.

*   *   *

GORDON STEPS ZIGZAG is an old beach approach once known as The Bunny and more often as Mount Misery. A girl signalling from here at night to guide smugglers is said to have thrown herself down the cliff when the boat overturned drowning her lover. However, the name may be due to the steep climb. Lady Bolingbroke, staying at Stourfield House about 1812, often had to be hauled up on a rope by a farmer much to the amusement of her husband, a keen fisherman who also found the climb difficult. Clifton Road behind was the old track to the beach access.

*   *   *

E9   *Here the E9 goes down the zigzag and along the promenade to its far end.*

The original coast path route continues on the cliff. At the top of the slope beyond the zigzag, the path narrows. Soon the path turns sharply left to join the road. Turn right to follow Southbourne Overcliff Drive, which has no sea view for almost ¼ mile, to reach the roundabout at Southbourne.

*   *   *

SOUTHBOURNE, once known as Southbourne-on-Sea, was named by Dr Thomas Compton who in 1870 bought the open area of gorse and sand to build a resort. Then the only buildings were Stourcliffe House, dating from the 1840s, and in Ken Road, and Cellars Farm. The coastguard cottages were built in 1873. Southbourne was thought to be more bracing than Bournemouth and suitable for asthma sufferers as it was more exposed and open to the winds from the Avon and Stour valleys. Another doctor recommended 'the absolutely unimpeded exposure to breezes and sunshine'. St Katharine's church, built in 1881–2, owes its dedication to Dr Compton who was inspired by the proximity of St Catherine's Hill and the sight of St Catherine's Point beyond the Needles on the Isle of Wight. By the end of the 19th century storm damage had closed the pier and caused the dismantling of houses built along the promenade. Slavanka in Belle Vue Road (near Avon Cliff Road junction) was, from 1877, the seaside home of Elizabeth Tchertkoff of St Petersburg who stayed permanently after the 1917 Russian Revolution until her death in 1921.

In the 1890s, the poet James Elroy Flecker spent his childhood holidays at a house on the site of Greenways, at the north end of Warren Edge Road. He described the pine trees as 'dark militia of the southern shore' in his poem *Brumana*. Angela Brazil based characters in *A Patriotic Schoolgirl* on her sister-in-law and nephew who lived on the top floor above the parade of shops in St Catherine's Road. Shell House, completed in 2004 near the roundabout, replaces the Shell Garden attraction which was there from 1948 until 2001.

*   *   *

E9   *In winter turn left at the roundabout for bus services to Bournemouth, Boscombe and Christchurch.*

Go right down the cliff to rejoin the E9 or visit Bistro on the Beach.

The main route continues along Southbourne Coast Road. Later there is Ferry Road (left) where the coastguard cottages can be found. The coast road runs gently downhill as the cliff loses height. The last house is Point House Café.

E9   *Here the E9 joins the road from the promenade.*

Walk 5
SOUTHBOURNE TO MUDEFORD – SUMMER ROUTE

The way is over Hengistbury Head for panoramic views of the coast and Christchurch Harbour. On the far side the path is along a beach, lined with coveted beach huts, to where a ferry carries walkers to Mudeford. The ferry operates daily from 10 am to at least 5 pm during British Summer Time and some winter weekends. See page 56 for the alternative winter route. The ferry can be contacted on 07968 334441.

DISTANCE: 2¼ miles

TRANSPORT: In summer Yellow Buses coastal service 12 runs to Bournemouth and Boscombe Piers. In winter the nearest bus services are in Belle Vue Road just inland from the clifftop roundabout (see page 50).

The beach at Hengistbury Head

REFRESHMENTS: Point House Café at the start is open daily from 10 am to 5.30 pm in summer. On the Mudeford Sandbank there is The Hut shop and café open daily in summer to 6 pm and winter weekends.

Point House Café on the edge of Southbourne is the very last house on the descending Poole Bay cliff. Here, where the road bears away from coast, leave the pavement and go ahead along the low cliff top. Stay on the path winding through sand dunes to pass the south end of Double Dykes.

DOUBLE DYKES may have been built in the Iron Age to protect a headland settlement. In the 1890s poet Elroy Flecker often wandered here and, around this time, a bridge was slung between the two banks for

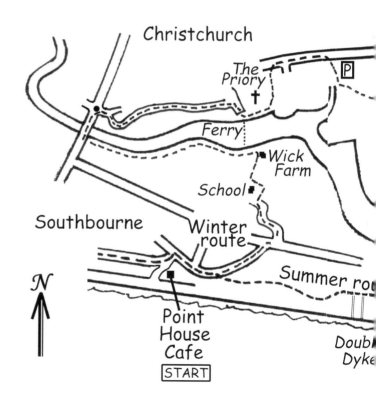

army training. Late in the 20th century erosion at the southern end was as rapid as four feet a year and this led to building the sea defence by the beach and a tough protection policy.

✽   ✽   ✽

Follow the path which soon winds up the hill to the viewpoint at the top of Hengistbury Head.

✽   ✽   ✽

HENGISTBURY HEAD affords a magnificent view of Christchurch Harbour, Christchurch Bay and Poole Bay. Around 100 BC this spot was

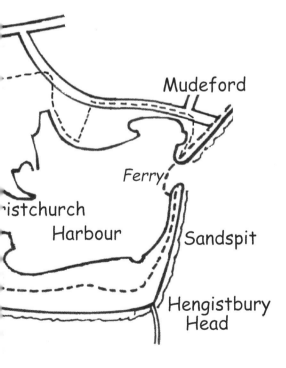

Hengistbury Head

Britain's largest port for European goods including Italian wine. The decline came with the arrival of the Romans and the area reverted to nature. Early in the last century the headland was bought by Gordon Selfridge, founder of the Oxford Street store, who employed architect Philip Tilden to design a mansion. But after the 1929 stock market crash, the plan fell through and the following year the land was purchased by Bournemouth Corporation. This is one of the busiest staging posts on the coast for migrating birds who use the Avon valley as a European gateway. The coastguard lookout, which was a wooden hut until 1975, has a view of the dangerous Beerpan Rocks where the French barque *Marie Thérèse* ran aground in 1899.

Walk ahead on the gravel path which runs past the coastguard lookout. Where the main path swings left keep ahead on the path which follows the cliff (right). Keep to the right at a second fork to pass high above the top of a lake (left). Keep on the main gravel way which avoids the edge of the cliff to reach a seat at the most easterly

point. Follow a stony and partly stepped way downhill to the huts on the Sandspit.

* * *

SANDSPIT The first beach huts appeared here in 1929 and now, occupied from March to November, there are around 350 of the country's most expensive huts. Access is only by boat or land train. At the end, opposite Mudeford Quay, is the Black House which was erected in the 1750s as a sail loft and accommodation for shipbuilders. Beyond here the sand bar turns north-east but its length varies every year. In 1880 there was a build-up of sand creating a mile long channel out of the harbour to the Highcliffe Castle beach. This was maintained until March 1935 when a storm suddenly reduced it to the original and now current length.

* * *

A sandy path runs along one side of the huts to join a metalled road used by the land train. At the terminus still keep forward on the beach to the pier just before the shop. Cross the Christchurch Harbour entrance to Mudeford by ferry.

* * *

MUDEFORD FERRY, linking the Mudeford Sandbank to Mudeford Quay, is operated by former P&O staff captain and local-born Paul Derham who has seen a rowing boat superseded by a motor vessel. The ferry runs, weather permitting, every 12 minutes from at least 10 am to 6 pm during the summer. (Tel: 07968 334441; www.mudefordferry.co.uk)

Walk 5
SOUTHBOURNE TO MUDEFORD – WINTER ROUTE

This route, open all year but the only option in winter, follows a route to Wick on the River Stour where there is a ferry and a nearby bridge. The way is then a mainly waterside walk through Christchurch, passing close to its landmark priory church, to cross Stanpit Marsh. This alternative route, although necessitated by the winter closure of Mudeford Ferry, is a rewarding and enjoyable diversion.

DISTANCE: 5 miles

TRANSPORT: In summer Yellow Buses coastal service 12 runs to Bournemouth and Boscombe Piers. In winter the nearest bus services are in Belle Vue Road just inland from the clifftop roundabout (see page 50).

REFRESHMENTS: Point House is open daily from 10 am to 5.30 pm in summer (see page 41); The Riverside Inn at Tuckton Bridge is open all day and there are plenty of cafés in Christchurch.

Christchurch Priory seen from Wick meadows

From Point House follow the road to St Nicholas' church.

* * *

ST NICHOLAS' CHURCH, designed in 1959 by architects Jackson & Greenen, was eventually completed in 1971. Appropriately, the dedication of this church near river and sea is to the protector of sailors. And it is here, in the modern setting, that the ancient custom is maintained of choosing a Boy Bishop on St Nicholas' Day.

* * *

Turn right and then left into Rolls Drive where there is a view of Christchurch Priory.

* * *

ROLLS DRIVE commemorates Rolls-Royce founder Charles Rolls who in 1910 died when his plane crashed on the edge of Southbourne during the Bournemouth Centenary Aviation Meeting. He was the first English air victim.

* * *

Follow Rolls Drive round the double bend and go right by the golf course entrance marked 'no entry' for cars. Walk along the bank on the right to pass the Solent Meads Golf Centre. Bear left by the seat to follow the back fence of a school. At the far end turn right and follow the path downhill. Ignore the 'Wick Village & Ferry' sign and keep ahead to reach a gate leading to a meadow on the edge of Wick.

* * *

WICK, having no pub or church, has always been a hamlet rather than a village. For a long time Wick Farm, with its cows, was the centre of life and cattle still graze on the meadows. Wick Farm House in the main street dates from at least 1770. Two old cottages on the green are the semi-detached Quality and Tranquility – the latter was the shop. The once-thatched 17th-century Riverside Cottage is near the ferry which has operated regularly across the River Stour to the Christchurch bank since 1814.

*　　*　　*

Go through the kissing gate and bear left on the curving path to a gap where the Stour Valley Way joins from the right. Go through the gap and turn left to another kissing gate. Follow the enclosed path to a final kissing gate leading to an expanse of grass by the River Stour. Follow the river (right) to join a path and reach Wick Ferry. Cross the river to Christchurch.

*　　*　　*

WICK FERRY runs Easter to October, 10 am to 5 pm; and winter on Saturday to Monday 10 am to 4 pm.

*　　*　　*

(If, due to being a winter weekday or bad weather, the ferry is not operating walkers should continue along the riverside at Wick to reach Tuckton Tea Gardens. Stay by the water to join a road opposite the Riverside pub. Turn right to cross Tuckton Bridge and go right into Willow Drive. After a few yards turn right into Willow Way. Follow this lane, which soon runs parallel to the main road, to a junction. Go right to reach the riverside and Wick Ferry.)

*　　*　　*

At Wick Ferry's Christchurch landing bear right on to The Quomps to follow the widening River Stour (right) downstream. Keep along the quayside and at the end go forward to pass the priory's mill (right).

*　　*　　*

PLACE MILL, mentioned in the Domesday Book, was Christchurch Priory's mill and continued to operate until 1908.

To visit the priory church go through a narrow gateway on the left.

* * *

CHRISTCHURCH PRIORY CHURCH, over a quarter of a mile long, is England's longest parish church and also has the longest porch. Building here, at the confluence of the rivers Avon and Stour, began in 1094 to a design by Durham Cathedral's main architect Ranulf Flambard. At this time the Saxon name changed from Twynham to 'Christ's Church' after a mysterious carpenter assisted with building work. A beam was found to be too short but next morning workmen discovered that it had grown to the correct length and been placed in position. As the carpenter did not reappear he was assumed to have been Christ. The Augustinian priory was closed by Henry VIII in 1539 but the town managed to save the church. Preserved inside is the magnificent chantry of Margaret, Countess of Salisbury, mother of Cardinal Reginald Pole, the last Roman Catholic Archbishop of Canterbury. Between 1857 and 1883 Canon Zachary Nash, great uncle of artist Paul Nash (see page 13), was curate and then vicar.

* * *

The walk continues to the right over the millstream. At once go left to follow the stream with the water on the left. There is a good view of the Priory and later the waterside Constable's House.

* * *

CONSTABLE'S HOUSE, with its rare chimney stack, was part of 13th-century Christchurch Castle whose ruined keep can be seen on the artificial mound behind. The King's Arms was built in 1801.

* * *

At the road go right over Town Bridge on to an island in the River Avon where the road becomes Bridge Street. Keep on the left-hand side to cross Waterloo Bridge.

At the Civic Centre turn right to go down the right-hand side of the building. Avoid the footpath which goes straight on and instead bear left round the back of the building. At the junction with Stoney

Lane go right into the car park and walk to the far left-hand corner. Go through the gateway to follow a path hugging a high bank.

Having crossed Purewell Stream follow the metalled path along the back of Stanpit Marsh.

*   *   *

STANPIT MARSH is a series of marshes which are home to many insects and butterflies, and over 250 species of birds and 300 plants in freshwater and saltmarshes. It is also a staging post for migrating birds. Grazing ponies are a reminder of the time when the New Forest ponies wandered as far as the coast. Appropriately, since it was invented in Christchurch, a Bailey bridge carries a path across Mother Siller's Channel, an inlet named after Hannah Siller who, in the 1780s, lived at the Ship in Distress pub in Stanpit and welcomed the smugglers using this remote landing spot. The MCC Museum at Lord's in London has a painting showing cricket being played here in 1849.

*   *   *

The way bends and eventually meets a car park at Stanpit. Bear right to the far corner and turn right along the road. After a short distance there is Well Cottage next to the grass site of Tutton's Well.

*   *   *

TUTTON'S WELL, where pilgrims visiting Christchurch Priory once stopped to bathe their eyes in the pure water, was known to the Romans. It was covered over in 1941.

*   *   *

Just beyond Victoria Road (left) go right to a footpath, known as Fisherman's Bank, running along the edge of Christchurch Harbour at the back of the cottages. Pass the end of Argyll Road and just as the waterside bends at a boatyard go left at an easily-missed turning. The path running inland bends four times before meeting the end of Coast Guard Way.

Walk to the far end and, opposite a recreation ground, go right along the main road to reach the centre of Mudeford.

MUDEFORD, originally 'Muddiford', takes its name from the River Mude which rises at Hinton Admiral and once flowed across the main street. Mudeford House was built in 1789 and the Avonmouth Hotel dates from 1818. Coleridge stayed in the village in 1816 when visiting fellow poet Robert Southey at Burton. The 1851 postbox is one of only three in the country. All Saints' church was designed by J.L. Pearson and was opened in 1869.

Walk past the Nelson, Mudeford House and the church before crossing the easily-missed River Mude and passing the shops. At the postbox go right to reach Mudeford Quay.

Walk 6
MUDEFORD TO MILFORD-ON-SEA

This, the last stretch of the Bournemouth Coast Path, follows the length of Christchurch Bay. However, crumbling cliffs require a new brief diversion at Chewton Bunny. Early on, the path passes through the grounds of Highcliffe Castle which writer Simon Jenkins describes as 'an architectural phenomenon'. After Barton-on-Sea, where teashops are among the few buildings not to have fallen with the cliff, the coast is more remote as the path is carried over Becton Bunny and down into Taddiford Gap. There are good views of the Isle of Wight and ships calling at Southampton.

DISTANCE: 8 miles
TRANSPORT: Wilts & Dorset buses 121, 122 and 123 link to Bournemouth and
       Christchurch.

Becton Bunny

REFRESHMENTS: There is an inn and a café on Mudeford Quay; a café on Avon Beach, open daily in summer and on winter Sundays; Highcliffe Castle tea room; and teashops at Barton-on-Sea.

MUDEFORD QUAY The 17th-century Dutch House, once occupied by Dutch dredging experts, was the original Haven House Inn. The present inn dates from the 1830s. The fish stall is open all year. Salmon, lobster, crab, whiting and mackerel are the main catches. A heavy herring catch in autumn indicates a cold winter. Christchurch salmon is netted in The Run between February and July. The most fruitful year was 1886 when 1,443 salmon were caught but now, due to increased boating traffic, the fish tend no longer to lie near the surface. Christchurch monks had the right to the first salmon.

✳   ✳   ✳

Walk along the quay, passing the fish stall and café, with the water to the right. Keep ahead on the wide metalled path. To the left is the caravan park in front of Sandhills.

Mudeford

SANDHILLS, built in 1785 and described as a 'cottage on the beach', was the home of George Rose, Christchurch MP and a friend of Nelson who stayed here. George III embarked from here on the Royal Yacht in the summer of 1801 with the queen and princesses for Weymouth. He called in again on his way back in October. In 1812 future Prime Minister George Canning stayed with his children for a holiday.

✳ ✳ ✳

Just before the end of the wide path, and on the corner of the main street, there is a good view of Gundimore.

✳ ✳ ✳

GUNDIMORE was built in 1796 for 21-year-old William Stuart Rose, younger son of George Rose of nearby Sandhills. The house is designed like an ancient Persian tent and inside the walls had deep red painted drapes edged with gold. Visitors included the exiled Louis Philippe and

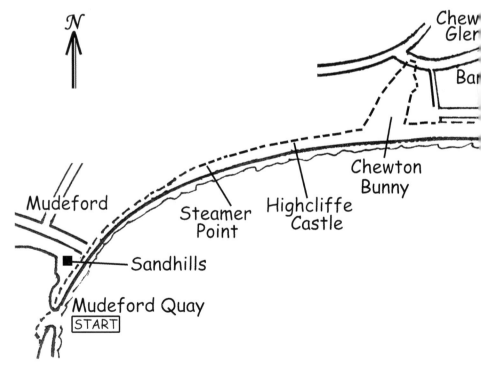

poets Coleridge, Southey and Ugo Foscolo. In 1807 Sir Walter Scott stayed here whilst writing *Marmion*.

✳   ✳   ✳

Ahead is the end of a road running inland to Mudeford village. Turn left into the road for a few yards before turning right and following a footpath to the top of a low cliff. Later a flight of wooden steps leads to a phone box and Avon Beach Café.

✳   ✳   ✳

AVON BEACH has been owned by the same family since 1929. The beach café and shop (open daily in summer and on Sundays in winter) are the successors to the boat moored here before the First World War which served refreshments to passing walkers. The building was first erected in 1925 but had to be rebuilt after Second World War

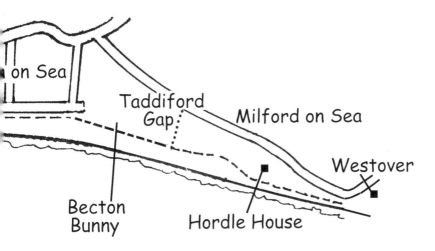

damage. It is now one of the best newsagents and bookshops on the coast path.

*   *   *

After a short distance Avon Run Road joins from the left as the cliff-top path continues under a long line of leaning pine trees. Where the road swings away to the left keep ahead down a slope to join a narrow footpath behind the beach huts. On reaching the toilets go left inland and at once right on the grass. Go down and up steps to reach Steamer Point.

*   *   *

STEAMER POINT is where Friars Cliff is low enough to allow easy beach access and here stone from France was landed for Highcliffe Castle. 'Friars' may refer to the monks of Christchurch Priory whilst 'Steamer' recalls the steamer which Lord Stuart de Rothesay of Highcliffe Castle beached here in 1835 and used as a beach hut. This was succeeded by Steamer Cottage until damaged by a storm in the 1940s. Another landmark here was a 60-ft high plastic Radome used for satellite communications from 1966 to 1980.

*   *   *

Continue eastwards through a clifftop gate and on to the rapidly rising cliff to pass the coastguard training school. On entering Steamer Point Woods, where there is a spectacular view west, the path enters the trees.

*   *   *

STEAMER POINT WOODS, opened to the public in 1984, was part of Highcliffe Castle's grounds laid out by 'Capability' Brown. Once overgrown with sycamore and rhododendrons, the woods have recently been thinned leaving a belt on the cliff top to act as a windbreak. The holly-leaved oaks are an important staging post for migrating birds. The woods' gateways are closed at dusk until 7 am.

*   *   *

Follow the main path through the wood and at a fork keep left. At the T-junction go right on a path which curves to run over open ground near the clifftop. Go through the gateway into Rothesay Wood to reach Common Gate leading to Highcliffe Castle.

*　　*　　*

HIGHCLIFFE CASTLE, originally just High Cliff, was said in the 1820s to have 'one of the most beautiful sea views in the kingdom'. The first house, designed by Robert Adam, was built on this site in the 1770s for former premier Lord Bute who would often come 'for the express purpose of obtaining sleep which he declared he could find here when it was to be had no where else'. The present castle was completed 100 yards north in 1835 for Bute's grandson, Lord Stuart de Rothesay, who incorporated parts of foreign buildings seen on his diplomatic travels. The oriel window on the south side comes from the room in the Grande Maison des Andelys in Normandy, where the King of Navarre died in 1562. The huge north portico contains an arch and cloister corbels from nearby Jumièges Abbey. Carved wooden panelling brought from France for the Great Hall is now in the Metropolitan Museum in New York.

Lord Stuart's daughter, Lady Waterford, inherited the property in 1845 and entertained numerous members of the royal family here. Queen Marie Amelie of France came in 1859, Queen Sophia Matilda of The Netherlands in 1872 and the Crown Prince of Sweden (the future Gustav V) in 1879. In 1880 the Prince of Wales (Edward VII) arrived on the royal yacht and the future George V had a swim. The Prince of Wales, accompanied by members of the German royal family, dropped in twice during the following year for tea and ice creams. Ten years later the royal yacht returned to take Lady Waterford to see Queen Victoria at Osborne on the Isle of Wight. Another guest at Highcliffe was William Gladstone, who came for a weekend in 1889 when Leader of the Opposition.

In 1891 the Castle was inherited by Major Edward Stuart Wortley and that year he welcomed the Duke of Connaught and future suffragette Ethel Smythe. In 1900 the future Edward VII became the first member of the royal family to be photographed in a car when he posed with Lord Montagu at the front of the building. In 1906 King Alfonso of Spain landed from the royal yacht, but the tree he planted died from no obvious cause just before his abdication in 1931. The last royal visitor in the 20th

Highcliffe Castle

century was Queen Mary who called in 1935 whilst staying at Wimborne St Giles. When Gordon Selfridge, the Oxford Street store founder, rented the Castle in 1916 he entertained tea merchant Sir Thomas Lipton.

The most significant visit was paid by the Kaiser who stayed for three weeks in 1907 following his state visit. Catering arrangements were in the hands of the 'Duchess of Duke Street' Rosa Lewis, who brought food down daily from London to Hinton Admiral station. The Kaiser told his host Major Stuart Wortley that the English were 'as mad as March hares' in not acknowledging him as their best friend. Later publication of these remarks in the *Daily Telegraph* caused a storm in the Reichstag, and calls for the Emperor's abdication. His chancellor, who had been at Highcliffe, failed to stand by him and at the declaration of the First World War, the Kaiser found his influence reduced. The first secretary of the Austrian embassy was dining here when he received a telegram announcing the assassination of Archduke Ferdinand at Sarajevo which precipitated the war.

When the Stuart Wortley family left in 1950, the Castle, incorporating stone from French Benedictine houses, became a seminary. Two serious fires and much argument reduced the building to a ruin. Its restoration was marked with a visit by the Duke of Gloucester in 2001. It is open from April to December, 11 am to 5 pm (winter 4 pm).

❋   ❋   ❋

Continue ahead by the fence (right) to reach a lawn. To the left there is a view of the Castle. Bear half right to join a wide zigzag path running down the cliff. Keep ahead where the path divides to walk east down steps and along the bottom of the cliff. Just after groyne H5 take the left hand path which curves uphill. At the far end climb the steps to the top of the cliff.

Turn right along the clifftop. The path passes a car park and runs down steps to cross the end of Waterford Road which links Highcliffe to the sea.

❋   ❋   ❋

HIGHCLIFFE In 1800 there were just a few houses and the village was called Slop Pond. By the 1830s new residents objected to the name and the growing community was called Newtown. This popular name caused such confusion that in 1892 the name of the Castle was adopted. St Mark's church was built in 1843 by Lord Stuart de Rothesay who is buried in its crypt. In 1926 Castle guest Dame Nellie Melba sang Gounod's 'Ave Maria' from the organ-loft during evensong. Gordon Selfridge is buried against the fence on the west side of churchyard where the avenue, known as Ninepenny Avenue because in 1843 each tree cost 9d, is a continuation of the Castle drive from the original Adam gateway. Greystones in Waterford Road was designed by Arts and Crafts architect E.S. Prior, and was completed in 1913.

❋   ❋   ❋

Bear right to go down the cliff, past a seat and down steps to Chewton Bunny.

❋   ❋   ❋

CHEWTON BUNNY Here the coastal valleys are called 'bunny' rather than 'chine' (see Boscombe page 6). An early document calls this 'la bonye de chiueton'. 'Chewton' is derived from 'Cifa's Farm'. In Elizabeth

I's reign it was feared that the Spanish Armada might consider this an easy landing place. Chewton Mill, ¼ mile up the bunny, dates from the 1740s having replaced an earlier one owned by Christchurch Priory as early as 1250. It was powered by the Walkford Brook (now the Dorset-Hampshire boundary) running down from the New Forest and under the road bridge which, when rebuilt in 1901, was the country's first steel reinforced concrete bridge.

In 1780 Riding Officer John Bursey was inveigled from his Chewton cottage one night by the claim that a large cache of contraband had been found. His wife, mother of four children, discovered him murdered in the morning. Captain Marryat, who had once been in command of a ship searching this coast for smugglers, wrote much of *Children of the New Forest* whilst a guest of his brother at the 17th-century Chewton Glen House, now an award-winning hotel, above the main road. The thatched cottages on Chewton Common date from around the 17th century.

*   *   *

There is no coastal public right of way between Chewton Bunny and Barton-on-Sea. Indeed there have been dramatic cliff falls along this stretch which is occupied by Naish holiday park (see below). Continue up the Bunny to join another path. After a few yards bear left over a bridge and up steps to pass a seat. The path climbs up through woodland. Occasionally, the Walkford Brook can be seen below.

Just after passing above the mill, leave the now metalled way and go right to continue on a woodland path. At a divide keep right to see a waterfall before meeting the main Highcliffe-Lymington road.

Go right over the footbridge attached to the road bridge to enter Hampshire. To the left across the road is the long boundary fence of Chewton Glen and on the right is the entrance to Naish Hoburne Holiday Park.

*   *   *

NAISH HOBURNE HOLIDAY PARK is the former Naish Farm which may have existed as early as James I's reign. The chalet, lodge and caravan park developed from the renting out of two farm huts in the summer holidays. The red brick 18th-century farmhouse with an inglenook fireplace survives as the holiday village's Smugglers Retreat pub (www.hoburne.com).

*   *   *

Continue round the main road's double bend. Just before reaching the Chewton Glen lodge on the left, go right on a footpath. The short way runs between trees to join a residential road.

At a junction take the metalled footpath half left opposite. Stay on this path, which briefly runs alongside a road, to meet another road. Cross over to find the path continuing near Neacroft Close. Eventually the path bears sharp left and narrows to run along the end of Vectis and Purbeck Roads to reach Marine Drive.

Go ahead alongside the caravan park fence and bear left to follow the cliff top. Walk along the wide grass cliff top to pass the isolated white painted Cliff House Hotel (left) and go over a gravel path leading to the beach. After 300 yards, bear half left at a small car park to join the parallel road and reach Barton's shops.

*   *   *

BARTON-ON-SEA   The cliffside is famous for its 40-million-year-old fossils. Rock or clay of this same age anywhere in the world is known as Bartonian. In 1863 there were just nine cottages here including Thatched Cottage, built in 1750, on the corner of Dilly Lane and Grove Road which was the centre of old Barton recorded in the Domesday Book. The coastguard cottages in Barton Lane were built in 1868 with Windy Ridge Nursing Home as the Chief Coastguard's house. At this time New Forest ponies often wandered to the cliffs. Development started in the 1890s after the railway arrived at Milton. The 1917 memorial to Indian troops, the oldest First World War memorial, records in Urdu and English the time when the Barton Court Hotel was a convalescent depôt for Indian troops. The hotel, which advertised 'Golfers' Hot Lunches', was the victim of crumbling cliffs and all that remains is the parade of shops. Cliff Edge Café on the west side was abandoned in 1990 and demolished soon after. It was at a now-demolished bungalow in the 1930s that award-winning novelist Elizabeth Goudge wrote *Island Magic*.

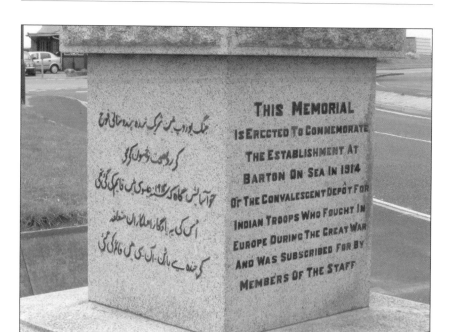

Barton-on-Sea's First World War memorial

The path continues along the cliff top. At the far end of Barton, go through two gates to continue along the cliff top with a golf course over to the left. The ground falls gently on approaching Becton Bunny. Before the bunny go left on a path which crosses the valley stream and runs along the far side.

BECTON BUNNY is still in its natural state with plenty of pink thrift in summer and a stream running over the beach into the sea – the once-familiar scene at all of Bournemouth's chines before the piping of water and planting of pines. As late as the 1860s, smuggled tubs of brandy were still being landed here at night.

*   *   *

Stay on the path as it continues along the cliff east of Becton Bunny with the golf course still inland. Soon the path starts to run downhill to a less dramatic valley known as Taddiford Gap.

*   *   *

TADDIFORD GAP, once used by smugglers, was defended by a line of concrete dragon's teeth placed here when this was believed to be a proposed landing area for the Germans during the Second World War. The few remaining teeth, still in place in the 1980s, have now fallen down the low cliff. 'Taddi' means 'toad' and 'ford' is a reference to the valley's Danes Stream.

*   *   *

The path climbs out of the valley to pass a trig point and follow the now less crumbling cliff where the way is bordered with thrift. Inland across the fields is Hordle House.

*   *   *

HORDLE HOUSE, an 18th-century building, was the home of Lord Justice Thesiger who died suddenly in 1880, at the age of 42 as a result of too much swimming. Until the 1940 invasion scare, the house had its own steps to the beach. The house was a school between 1926 and 1997 when pupils included film director Derek Jarman.

To the west of the house is the site of Hordle church which in 1829 was pulled down after the village was moved two miles inland due to the crumbling cliffs. The Norman church is depicted on a banner in the new church. Left behind in the old churchyard are the tombs of Sir Reginald de Clerk, who died in the Wars of the Roses, and Christopher Clark who died in 1720 aged 112. Other graves contain the bodies of shipwrecked sailors. In February 1818 there were nine bodies in the church awaiting burial after the 500 ton *True British Tar* was wrecked on its way back from Sierra Leone with a cargo of wood and ivory.

*   *   *

Where the farmland ends the cliff path becomes metalled and soon there are plenty of seats, a toilet and a tea hut. As the cliff loses height on approaching Milford-on-Sea there is a line of trees protecting Westover from sea winds.

*　　*　　*

WESTOVER was built in 1897 by electricity pioneer Alexander Siemens for his wife. The architect of this 'flamboyant piece of late-Victorian architecture' was Arnold Mitchell. Inside there is stained glass and rare William de Morgan tiles. After Siemens died here in 1928, the house became home of car manufacturer Lord Nuffield. The building is now Westover Hall hotel.

*　　*　　*

The path then runs below the large White House.

*　　*　　*

THE WHITE HOUSE was built in 1903 as a seaside home for the Walker-Munro family of Rhinefield House in the New Forest. Both buildings were

Milford Cliff

designed by Romaine Walker. In 1938 it became a children's hospital and is now divided into several residences.

*　　*　　*

Beyond is Milford-on-Sea promenade and the Needles Eye café where the Bournemouth Coast Path meets the Solent Way. Milford village centre lies inland at the end of Sea Road behind the café.

Walk 7
MILFORD-ON-SEA TO LYMINGTON

This section is the beginning of the Solent Way coast path. Early on, the path is briefly on the Hurst Spit, the long shingle bank which has recently been strengthened following the loss of 150,000 tons of shingle after a storm in 1989. It is an extra 3-mile walk to the castle at the end, and back; in 1866 William Morris declined to undertake the trek.

After Keyhaven there is a five mile twisting sea wall along lonely marshes where from at least 1191 to 1865 the salt industry maintained up to 200 pans. Sea water caught in ponds at high tide was allowed to partially evaporate in the sun before the brine was piped by wind pumps into boiling houses heated by coal. The last saltern closed after the railways started transporting salt from Cheshire. The few people found here today, apart from walkers, are bird watchers and locals digging for bait.

DISTANCE: 7 miles

TRANSPORT: Wilts & Dorset buses 123 and 124 link to Bournemouth and Lymington and stop by the shops in the centre of Milford-on-Sea. At Lymington there are trains which meet main-line Bournemouth–London Waterloo services at Brockenhurst.

REFRESHMENTS: The Needles Eye Café on the seafront is open daily in summer; and there is the Gun pub at Keyhaven, and teashops in Lymington.

MILFORD-ON-SEA The name means 'mill by a ford'. The mill is now a private house in Barnes Lane and the ford has been replaced by a bridge. The last miller, who left in 1899, grew his own corn and baked and delivered bread. The Norman church was served by monks from Christchurch Priory who slept beneath the lean-to roofs at the base of the tower. The present squat tower was added in 1827. In the chancel there is a stained-glass window showing Charles I who was held at nearby Hurst Castle. In 1866 William Morris visited the church followed the next year by Dante Gabriel Rossetti. On the western side of the churchyard is the grave of Sir Edgar Whitehead, the last but one prime minister of Southern Rhodesia.

During the 1801 Christmas morning sermon, the congregation saw

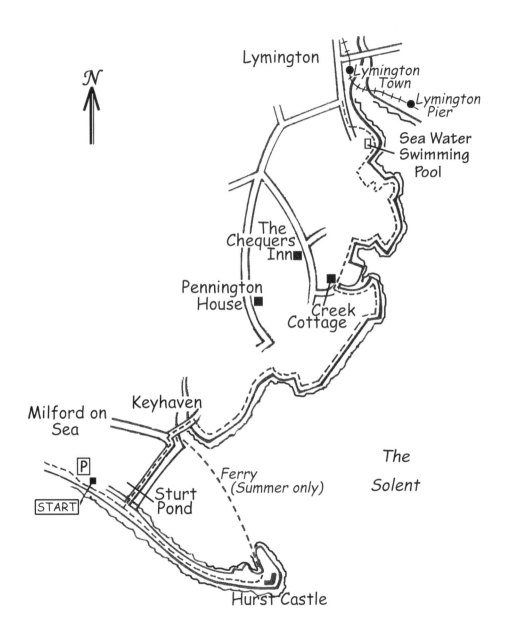

N

Lymington

Lymington
Town

Lymington
Pier

Sea Water
Swimming
Pool

The
Chequers
Inn

Pennington
House

Creek
Cottage

Keyhaven

Milford on
Sea

*Ferry
(Summer only)*

*The
Solent*

P

START

Sturt
Pond

Hurst Castle

Hurst Spit

through the north windows that Newlands Manor was on fire. One by one people left until the vicar paused to ask the verger where everyone had gone. The Georgian mansion was restored in its present gothic style and, later in the century, Colonel William Cornwallis-West entertained the Prince of Wales, the Kaiser and Lillie Langtry who were all friends of his wife Patsy. Their son George shocked society by marrying Winston Churchill's widowed mother whilst the daughters became the Princess of Pless and the Duchess of Westminster.

Turn eastwards at the Needles Eye Café to walk along the promenade and on to the shingle spit. Below, on the left inland, is Sturt Pond and a wooden bridge. Cross the second bridge, Sturt Bridge, spanning the Sturt Pond channel. Only continue ahead past the second bridge to visit Hurst Castle at the far end of the spit.

* * *

HURST SPIT & CASTLE The shingle spit, strengthened in recent years, was less firm when the castle was completed in 1544 as part of Henry

Milford Spit

VIII's defences. Charles I was held prisoner here for just over two weeks in 1648 before being taken to London for a show trial and execution on 30th January. From 1700 to 1729 Roman Catholic Franciscan Paul Atkinson was held here under penal laws. The Governor, taking advantage of the remoteness of the area, allowed his prisoner an occasional change of scene by taking him home to a nearby farm. In the monk's last years he was allowed to say mass for a Roman Catholic family at Everton Grange, two miles north of Keyhaven.

The castle's massive wings were added between 1860 and 1873. Alongside the castle are cottages, a lighthouse, the lighthouse keeper's house, and a pub, which is closed. The castle provides a good view of the Solent and Christchurch Bay, and is open daily between 1st April and the end of September, 10 am to 5.30 pm, and also in October from 10 am until 4 pm.

*   *   *

The main Solent Way route crosses the wooden Sturt Bridge. Follow the waterside road ahead for 350 yards and, just beyond a floodgate, keep ahead where the road bears away from the water. Go through a gateway onto a track. Across the reeds can be seen the chimneys of Salt Grass.

*At a T-junction, waymarked with the Solent Way's tern, go left on
to a short path to rejoin the road at a bend in Keyhaven.*

*   *   *

KEYHAVEN is mentioned as a port as early as 1206, although it is a
difficult harbour to enter. In the late 19th century the Prince of Wales used
to land here by launch from the royal yacht when visiting Newlands. A
carriage would wait for him outside the 17th-century Gun pub.
Tennyson's father-in-law rented Aubrey House in Keyhaven Road on the
recommendation of fellow poet William Allingham. Nearby Salt Grass is
built with stones brought from Beaulieu Abbey.

The Isle of Wight

*At the T-junction opposite the Gun, take the easterly road which
runs along the edge of the water and crosses a bridge. Turn right to
leave the road and follow a footpath along the shoreline. The
narrow stony way is mainly raised but occasionally joins the
beach. The path provides the nearest view of Hurst Castle from the
mainland. Across the Solent is the Isle of Wight and inland are the
Keyhaven Marshes – old salterns.*

Soon the way is along the top of a concrete sea wall and as the wall turns so the Isle of Wight's Needles are suddenly to the right rather than behind. After several turns the path runs in a north-easterly direction for almost a mile. Across the Solent is Yarmouth. Inland, peeping out of the trees on the far side of Pennington Marshes, is Pennington House.

* * *

PENNINGTON HOUSE is an early 18th-century house enlarged in 1923. It was the home of the Marquess of Headfort soon after his controversial marriage in 1901 to Rosie Boot, star of *Messenger Boy* at the Gaiety Theatre. The couple needed to economise and William and Patsy Cornwallis-West (see page 78) recommended the lonely house where the Headforts were visited by the Cornwallis-West's daughters, the Princess of Pless and the Duchess of Westminster. From 1951 until 1991 this was the home of Lord Lurgan whose family had owned the house since 1916.

* * *

Eventually the path begins to bear left up Oxey Lake - the entrance to an inlet. Lymington can be seen a mile away although by the twisting coast path it is over two miles.

The path, with various surfaces, continues bearing left until it is running in a south-westerly direction up the side of a narrow channel. Once there were oyster beds here. At a wooden stile, the path and water turn right and the now very narrow channel ends in front of Creek Cottage.

* * *

CREEK COTTAGE, which is mainly Victorian, stands at the head of a creek once known as Moses Dock and used by barges bringing coal for the salt boiling houses. One of the Tudor barns by the water may have been a boiling house whilst the other was probably for storage of salt which was weighed and sold at the nearby Chequers pub.

* * *

Quay Street, Lymington

(To reach the Chequers turn left before the Creek Cottage stile to follow an enclosed way to Ridgeway Lane and turn right.)

Climb over the wooden stile and turn right to pass between Creek Cottage (left) and the water. Continue forward leaving the water to pass through a long tunnel of trees. The straight path passes a row of former saltern cottages before becoming a metalled lane. Later there is Salterns Sailing Club (right) on the edge of Eight Acre Pond. Soon after passing Maiden Cottage (right) leave the lane (which turns left) and go right on a short gravel path to reach the sea.

Keep on the left side of the channel. After several twists and turns there is a view inland to Lymington's church tower. Soon the path turns towards the town and reaches the famous marina.

Keep left to follow a narrow path which soon runs along the edge of an inlet. At a fork keep right with the water. Later the path crosses the channel to enter a boatyard. Keep ahead on the fenced path and at a road go right and then left.

At the end, follow a path which runs between water (right) and the Sea Water Swimming Pool (left).

THE SEA WATER SWIMMING POOL was formerly called King's Saltern, after Lymington's bookseller Richard King who owned 22 pans here. This, the south coast's largest salt water baths, was once divided by a corrugated fence into male and female sections. King's bookshop in Lymington's High Street was opened in 1805 and is now Ottakar's.

✻   ✻   ✻

Follow the path round the corner to pass the slipway and the Royal Lymington Yacht Club (right). Keep by the waterside and, after passing a bandstand, go left on a path which passes a pond and joins the parallel Bath Road.

Turn right to continue into Lymington on this road which, beyond the Ship Inn on the quay (right), narrows to become Quay Street. At the end bear left up to the High Street. The Solent Way

Lymington Channel

continues to the right to pass Station Road which leads to Lymington town station.

*   *   *

LYMINGTON During Edward III's war with France, twice as many ships were built here as in Portsmouth. In 1648 the town supplied Prince Charles' ships which lay off Yarmouth in case Charles I could be rescued from Carisbrook. But 40 years later the mayor raised 100 men to support the Duke of Monmouth against James II. In 1789 George III and Queen Charlotte visited and today the Princess Royal is a frequent visitor as Patron of the Royal Lymington Yacht Club.

The Saturday market, started in the 13th century, takes place in the High Street which bends round the church also dating from this time. Its distinctive tower was erected in 1670 with the cupola added later. Henry Lyte, author of the hymn *Abide With Me*, was a curate from 1818 to 1823.

Thomas Rowlandson stayed at the Angel in 1784 and sketched the 'pretty landlady'. Until the 20th century, fire engine horses were stabled at the back and when the alarm rang the stable door would be opened to allow a horse to run on its own along the High Street to the fire station in Queen Street.

Port Colborne in Ontario is named after Sir John Colborne who was born here in 1778 when his father was a salt officer. Also born here was painter George Hicks whose father, a magistrate, appears in *Before The Magistrates* which was exhibited amid much comment at the Royal Academy in 1866. During the 1860s, poet William Allingham was the customs officer and described Lymington as 'the most Yachtish place in the world'. His poem *Laurence Bloomfield* was published in 1864 and, on opening *The Times* in the newsagents, he was thrilled to read that Gladstone had quoted from it in the House of Commons. Poet Coventry Patmore lived on the far side of Lymington River but still used to walk into town in his dressing gown. Author Dennis Wheatley lived at a (now demolished) house in Grove Road from 1944 until his death in 1968.

ACCOMMODATION

SWANAGE

Hermitage Guesthouse (in the town centre):
1 Manor Road BH19 2BH.
Tel: 01929 423014
www.hermitage-online.co.uk

The Limes Hotel (in the town centre):
48 Park Road BH19 2AE.
Tel: 01929 422664
www.limeshotel.demon.co.uk

Perfick Piece (opposite the station):
3 Springfield Road BH19 1HD.
Tel: 01929 423178

ALUM CHINE (Bournemouth West Cliff)

Lawnswood Hotel (on the Bournemouth Coast Path cliff top route; turn right just before the suspension bridge):
22a Studland Road BH4 8JA.
Tel: 01202 761170

Mount Lodge Hotel (on Bournemouth Coast Path cliff top route just before the suspension bridge):
19 Beaulieu Road BH4 8HY.
Tel: 01202 761173

BOURNEMOUTH

Bewdley Hotel (turn left at the side of the Highcliff Hotel):
70 St Michael's Road BH2 5DH.
Tel: 01202 553530

St Michael's Guest House (turn left at the side of the Highcliff Hotel):
42 St Michael's Road, West Cliff BH2 5DY.
Tel: 01202 557386
www.stmichaelsfriendlyguesthouse.co.uk

The Newark Hotel (turn left at the side of the Highcliff Hotel):
65 St Michael's Road BH2 5DP.
Tel: 01202 294989

BOSCOMBE

Denewood Hotel (walk up the hill from Boscombe Pier; the hotel is on
right at a crossroads):
40 Sea Road BH5 1BQ.
Tel: 01202 394493
www.denewood.co.uk

Valberg Hotel (walk east from Shelley Park):
1a Wollstonecraft Road BH5 1JQ
Tel: 01202 394644

CHRISTCHURCH

Druid House Hotel (continue north from Wick Ferry):
26 Sopers Lane BH23 1JE.
Tel: 01202 485615
www.druid-house.co.uk

STANPIT

Salmon's Reach (turn left at Stanpit):
28 Stanpit BH23 3LZ.
Tel: 01202 477315
www.salmonsreach.com

MUDEFORD

Seawards (walk to the back of the car park behind Avon Beach):
13 Avon Run Close BH23 4DT.
Tel: 01425 273188
www.seawards13.plus.com

HIGHCLIFFE CASTLE

Castle Lodge (behind Highcliffe Castle; turn right at the main road):
173 Lymington Road BH23 4JS.
Tel: 01425 275170
www.castlelodge-highcliffe.co.uk

HIGHCLIFFE

Sea Corner Guest House (turn left along Waterford Road above Chewton Bunny):
397 Waterford Road BH23 5JN.
Tel: 01425 272731
www.seacorner-guesthouse.co.uk

BARTON-ON-SEA

Everglades (behind Cliff House Hotel alongside coast path):
81 Sea Road BH25 7ND.
Tel: 01425 617350
www.evergladesbandb-newforest.co.uk

Laurel Lodge (on the left between Naish Holiday Park and Cliff House Hotel):
48 Western Avenue BH25 7PZ.
Tel: 01425 618309

MILFORD-ON-SEA

The Bay Trees (in centre of village):
8 High Street SO41 0QD.
Tel: 01590 642186

Ha'penny House (at far end of Cornwallis Road, on cliffs):
16 Whitby Road SO41 0ND.
Tel: 01590 641210
www.hapennyhouse.co.uk

LYMINGTON

Dolphins (off New Street near the Tourist Information Centre):
6 Emsworth Road SO41 9BL.
Tel: 01590 676108
www.dolphinsnewforestbandb.co.uk

Durlston House (near the station):
Gosport Street SO41 9EG.
Tel: 01590 677364
www.durlstonhouse.co.uk

SELECT BIBLIOGRAPHY

Ashley, Harry. *The Dorset Coast* (Countryside, 1992)

Edwards, Elizabeth. *Bournemouth Past* (Phillimore, 1998)

Hatts, Leigh. *The Fabians in Bournemouth* (Fabian Society, 1999)

Hodges, Michael A. *Christchurch* (Frith, 2001)

Legg, Rodney. *Old Swanage* (DPC, 1983)

Newman, John & Pevsner, Nikolaus. *The Buildings of England: Dorset* (Penguin, 1972)

Pevsner, Nikolaus & Lloyd, David. *The Buildings of England: Hampshire* (Penguin, 1967)

Young, David S. *The Story of Bournemouth* (SR Publications, 1970)

WEBSITES

Bournemouth Coast Path: www.bournemouthcoastpath.org.uk

Dorset Coast Forum: www.dorsetcoast.com

Dorset Coast Path: www.nationaltrail.co.uk

Long Distance Walkers Association: www.ldwa.org.uk

South West Coast Path Association: www.swcp.org.uk

Solent Way: www.hants.gov.uk/walking/solentway

TOURIST INFORMATION CENTRES

SWANAGE: The White House, Shore Road BH19 1LB.
Tel: 01929 422885
www.swanage.gov.uk

POOLE: Poole Welcome Centre, Enefco House, Poole Quay BH15 1HJ.
Tel: 01202 253253
www.pooletourism.com

BOURNEMOUTH: Westover Road BH1 2BU.
Tel: 0906 80 20 234
www.bournemouth.co.uk

CHRISTCHURCH: 3 High Street BH23 1AZ.
Tel: 01202 471780
www.resort-guide.co.uk/christchurch

LYMINGTON: St Barbe Museum & Visitor Centre, New Street SO41 9BH.
Tel: 01590 689000
www.thenewforest.co.uk

A London bollard in Swanage

INDEX

Index